MINDMELD

Micro-Collaboration between eLearning Designers and Instructor Experts

by Jon D. Aleckson and Penny Ralston-Berg

Megan —
I think you will find
we share a lot in common.
Here is to our future work
together!
Jon Alec
November, 2015

Atwood Publishing
Madison, Wisconsin

MindMeld: Micro-Collaboration between eLearning
Designers and Instructor Experts
by Jon D. Aleckson and Penny Ralston-Berg

Author's Note: All quotations in this book come from personal communications with Jon Aleckson unless otherwise indicated. They represent the views of the individuals to which they are attributed and are not necessarily endorsed by any people or programs affiliated with those individuals. Some quotations have been altered to increase their readability. Where the alterations are minor, especially where they are grammatical, no indication of the alteration is given in the text.

Library of Congress Cataloging-in-Publication Data

Aleckson, Jon D., 1956-
   MindMeld : micro-collaboration between eLearning designers and instructor experts / by Jon D. Aleckson and Penny Ralston-Berg.
      p. cm.
   Includes bibliographical references and index.
   ISBN 978-1-891859-85-4 (pb)
   1. Computer-assisted instruction—Design. 2. Internet in education. 3. Academic-industrial collaboration. I. Ralston-Berg, Penny, 1969- II. Title. III. Title: Mind meld.
   LB1028.5.A3575 2011
   371.33'44678—dc23
                              2011019565

To my wife Mary and our three children.
—Jon Aleckson

To my husband Rich.
—Penny Ralston-Berg

Acknowledgments

from Jon D. Aleckson

We put so much emphasis these days on preparing students for taking tests! I'm not a gifted test-taker, myself. So I must first thank those of my teachers who, early on, recognized that my talents came to the forefront when I was *doing* something that interested me. (At fourteen, for example, I was allowed to make an 8mm movie to satisfy my high school class requirements.) As I got older and came to a greater awareness of my learning faculties, I developed a commitment to educational technology, and the industry of educational technology has been the cornerstone of my professional life.

At the age of fifty (my low GRE score notwithstanding), the University of Wisconsin gave me the chance to research the ways in which people work together on eLearning projects. I came to an understanding of how teams can better create products that allow people to learn by doing, and this understanding led to my doctoral dissertation and the awarding of my PhD. So I'm indebted to those at the UW who believed in me personally, who recognized the value of my life experience and saw how I might contribute to our growing knowledge of online-learning development. Alan Knox guided me on a seven-year journey during which I came to focus on both evaluation practices and the nascent study of video games and learning principles. My work was also influenced by Kurt Squire, Rich Halverson, Betty Hayes, Don Hanna, Lori Bakken, and Carolyn Kelley, and I owe a lot to my fabulous dissertation editors, Catherine Cuddihee, Patty Haeger, and Maryanne Haselow-Dulin. All of these people have my immense respect and gratitude.

I would not have been able to write this book without the cooperation of the people at UW DoIT's Engage program, who have generously allowed me to use their efforts as illustrations of my theoretical model. On an individual basis, Christine Lupton's trust and guidance helped me reflect deeply on what became my central case study. John Pfotenhauer, Dave Gagnon, and Mike Litzkow, Les Howles, Brad Hughes, and Chris

Blakesley have lent me the authority of their words and submitted cheerfully to my questioning.

My academic journey has had a large impact on my private practice. I am pleased to say that my colleagues Dawn Smith, Andy Hicken, Aileen Zhang, Paul DelFino, Clark Aldrich, and Bill Horton have influenced not only this book, but many of the online projects in which I've played a part. I have learned from them all.

MindMeld went from an idea to a final manuscript in a matter of months. It hardly needs pointing out that this wouldn't have happened without a team of passionate and highly skilled individuals. There is of course my redoubtable co-author Penny Ralston-Berg, who has added a hugely important perspective for those in higher education. In academia's drive to transfer more and more of the classroom experience to the internet, Penny has worked on countless projects and been a tireless advocate for the learner. She can speak to every detail of dealing with curriculum teams and professors, and she knows how to get learners to problem-solve and interact with one another. Those who work with her find she has a natural facility for micro-collaboration.

My publisher Linda Babler has an incredibly calm and supportive attitude that helped us maintain not only our momentum, but also the level of academic quality that she demands of her titles. In addition, I owe a great deal of gratitude to my editor and co-writer Charles Hogle, who labored over every word of this book and whose prose adds substantially to our argument, particularly the articulation of my five factors. Charles has the sort of versatile expertise that you find in any field's rising stars.

Most important of all, I have benefitted profoundly from the continuous support of my parents and my wife, Mary, all of whom have helped me see that I belong to a literal family of educators.

A commitment to lifelong learning ignites new passions on an individual level, and it has done great things for me. But at root, learning isn't something we do as individuals. Rather, learning is a social endeavor, and it is so much more fun when shared by people who are good at what they do—people who help you accomplish things you could never have accomplished by yourself.

—*Jon Aleckson, April 2011*

from Penny Ralston-Berg

In a world of shrinking academic budgets, the ideas of "quantity" and maximizing online enrollments too often overshadow the potential for quality in online courses. Quality does not happen by accident. It is something that must be held as a goal from the very start of a project and integrated into the development process. It takes time, a diverse team, supportive management, and the ability to see things from a learner point of view. An engaged and knowledgeable instructor-expert is part of that team.

Instructor-experts Amy Dietz, Kim Kostka, and Sarah Davis have my deepest respect and serve as models of effective practice through their openness, willingness to actively participate in the design process and commitment to quality—to ensure learners get the most from online learning experiences. I appreciate them taking time to share their experiences and thoughts with us to illustrate the model.

I appreciate my co-author's dedication to improving micro-collaboration between designers and instructor-experts. Jon Aleckson's research and Five Factors model encourage effective micro-collaboration in all phases of a project—combining design and production with communication, momentum, and soft skills not often taught in design programs. It has been a pleasure to turn the tables and become an "instructor-expert" for a brief period of time. The whole experience has helped me become a better designer and I thank him for the opportunity.

My participation in this book would not have been possible without the encouragement and patience of my husband, Rich. His support and understanding inspire me. I am also thankful to Mary Grant for being a voice of reason and encouragement over the years. Also, to my design colleagues past and present, thank you for keeping me in a constant state of learning. I would not be where I am today if not for the people in my life. As life long learners we will all continue to explore, investigate, challenge, test, collaborate and grow.

—*Penny Ralston-Berg, April 2011*

Table of Contents

Foreword

By Clark Aldrich

In reading *MindMeld*, I am struck by four dyads, or pairs of complementary truths. Taken together, these dyads constitute not the book's theory, but its ethos.

The first one is this: learning involves both knowing and doing. Academic courses lean toward the former while business courses lean toward the latter, but sophisticated online learning should span both realms. Accordingly, any book purporting to address online learning as a whole must speak to both, as the authors of *MindMeld* are well aware. Jon Aleckson has spent thirty years developing educational technology in the private sector; he has molded that experience into a theoretical framework that he devised during his doctoral research at the University of Wisconsin-Madison. Penny Ralston-Berg has spent fourteen years designing online educational tools in a variety of higher-education settings; she is now at the vanguard of of the field. Therefore, in combination, Jon and Penny are able to see online learning from a multivalent perspective.

Second: great people need great processes, and great processes need great people. I have immense respect for Jon's ability to recognize this dyad in his professional life. He finds and embraces the most talented people out there, then allows their talent to flourish by giving them the right work environment. The capacity for doing this should be considered a prerequisite for anyone involved in technology-based education, but it's quite rare, and is in fact quite difficult to keep up day in and day out. So I am happy— though not surprised—to see this skill reflected in *MindMeld*.

Third, this book blends the scholarly and the practical. It cites critical and current research in the field, but readers will certainly be able to tell that the authors have some coal under their fingernails (so to speak). This junction is precious not only because it is rare, but because both elements can and must complement each other. We have all seen academics who spend money like water, toil for years, and produce remarkably little—just as we have seen practitioners who ignore critical theory, make stuff up as they go along, spurn reflection, and try to do as little as possible for as much as possible. This book exemplifies the good qualities of both worlds while skirting their many traps.

The fourth dyad speaks to a major issue: the role of the subject matter expert, or SME. For reasons they explain later on, the authors refer to SMEs as "instructor-experts," so I'll adopt their terminology. Instructor-experts occupy a strange place in any technology-based development process. They are not the captains of the ship, nor should they be; but often, they are not even treated as precious cargo. Indeed, they're sometimes treated as ballast. In other words, they are seen as problems for instructional design teams to solve.

Why is it so important to change this state of affairs? Because we know that instructor-experts make or break the content of any online learning program; we know that no program can exceed the wisdom or erudition of the instructor-expert who works on it. *MindMeld* provides strategies for integrating instructor-experts into the development process—strategies, that is, for making sure that instructor-experts' time and knowledge are respected on the personal and organizational levels.

Helping instructional design and development specialists understand the instructor-expert's role is one element of the fourth dyad. While reading this book, the other element of the dyad becomes clear: *MindMeld* will prompt instructor-experts to see their own thinking in a new light. In effect, they will increase their value as technology-based learning partners—not only because they will understand the development process, but because they will understand how their own *ways* of thinking fit into that process. To put it differently, this book will help instructor-experts escape the trap of having to spend so much time explaining themselves that they become curators of increasingly dated knowledge, rather than explorers of new frontiers.

The four dyads that make up *MindMeld*'s ethos are academia and the private sector, good people and good processes, critical theory and personal experience, and instructional design and development and subject-matter expertise. The authors have incorporated all of these dyads into their model. This makes their perspective rare and invaluable, and I hope that everyone in our industry will embrace it.

Clark Aldrich (one of Fortune *magazine's global education "gurus") is an award-winning industry analyst, speaker, and author. His patented simulations have generated millions in revenues and are market leaders in their categories.*

Introduction

Online learning is rapidly moving from the realm of the familiar to the realm of the commonplace, and will soon enter the realm of the fully expected. This isn't breaking news: people have been talking about it for years. So why go into it? Because there's more to online learning's prevalence than quantitative growth: online learning is undergoing a change in its very nature—a qualitative leap from one stage of evolution to the next.

Our book is about small teams using sophisticated technology to create immersive and highly interactive learning objects; it is this immersive interactivity that distinguishes today's online learning from the online learning that came before. More to the point, what's qualitatively special about the new breed of online learning is that it can give people the same sort of experience they'd get in the lab or in the field. It can give people the chance to *learn by doing*, to accumulate what amounts to real-world know-how. Online learning has advanced so much that it's now commensurate with other, more traditional species of pedagogy, and—when it's done right—can dramatically reduce the amount of time and resources required to turn someone from a novice into an expert.

Of course, it's all well and good to gesture toward online learning's fascinating and revolutionary *potential*. But it's not enough. This book is meant as a guide for practitioners in corporations, associations, nonprofits, and academic institutions, and so we need to provide concrete methods of turning the potential into the *actual*. Otherwise, we'd be writing speculative fiction.

Speculative fiction isn't our business. Rather, we specialize in *strategy*. We've been working in the online learning industry for decades: we've seen a lot of what works and a lot of what doesn't. Our jobs require us to get results. Therefore, we'll be talking not only about what online learning *can* be, but also about *how to get there*.

Micro-collaboration

As we mentioned, our focus is on the small teams that are tasked with designing and developing online learning objects. In order to generate immersive, highly interactive learning objects, these teams must contain people of very different backgrounds with very different skills; i.e., instructional designers, software developers, graphic artists, project managers, editors, media specialists, and instructor-experts. To achieve educational outcomes, teams must perform a complex balancing act in which their members simultaneously teach and learn from one another.

This mutually instructive balancing act lies at the heart of *micro-collaboration*. We attach the prefix "micro" here in order to distinguish *interpersonal* collaboration from interdepartmental or inter-organizational collaboration. The latter forms involve large bureaucratic entities, and while they're important, they're also fairly grand and abstract. By contrast, micro-collaboration occurs between individuals. It is detailed and particular.

Small teams working on interactive learning objects need to micro-collaborate if they want to realize the full potential of online pedagogy. The purpose of online pedagogy is to impart real-world know-how using the tools of software design, and for that to happen, instructional design and development (IDD) experts need to work in concert with instructor-experts. Instructor-experts (also known as subject-matter experts, or SMEs) *already* have real-world experience in the content domain, and can *teach* the instructional design and development people what learners need to know. Reciprocally, it's up to IDD experts to teach instructor-experts how online learning differs from in-class, face-to-face learning and thus demands a different approach.

This teaching/learning transaction between IDD experts and instructor-experts is, for us, the heart and soul of micro-collaboration. It's what makes the difference between talking about the *potential* of online learning and turning that potential into *reality*.

Without strong micro-collaboration, the chances of developing a high-quality interactive learning object are slim indeed. That's why understanding micro-collaboration is so important. What this book provides is a conceptual framework that demystifies micro-collaboration by dividing it into five factors: politics, structure, culture, performance, and momentum. The framework is based largely on Jon Aleckson's doctoral research at the University of Wisconsin-Madison; it is supported by Jon Aleckson's thirty years of leading educational technology development in the private sector and Penny Ralston-Berg's fourteen years of experience as an instructional designer in academia. It represents a blend of theory and personal practice.

In the interest of explaining our model and laying the groundwork for upcoming chapters, we'll take a moment to discuss our terminology and outline our argument.

Interactive Learning Objects (ILOs)

"Interactive learning object," or "ILO," is our generic term for any online activity that demands some input from the user in order to function—basically, anything more complicated than a simple, "watch this video, read this article" format. That leaves a lot of room for interpretation, and it's

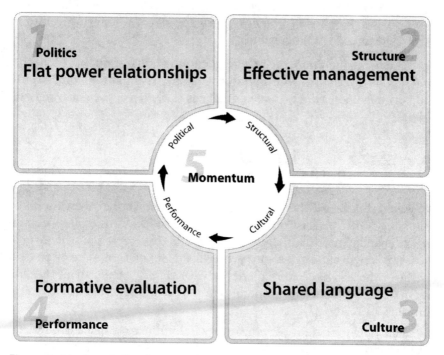

Figure 1: Aleckson's five factors of micro-collaboration.

meant to: we see every ILO as falling somewhere on a grid, or Cartesian plane, with the plane's axes being "implementation" and "design." Each axis is a continuum: the "x" axis goes from simple design to complex design, and the "y" axis goes from simple implementation to complex implementation. The continuums bisect each other. When seen in this light, every ILO can be graphed according to two values: the complexity of its design and the complexity of its implementation.

Some ILOs are simple, some are advanced, and there are many, many of them out there. The ubiquity of software-authoring programs makes it possible for just about anyone with a few basic skills to come up with a crude ILO; our argument is that the same technological progress that's made software-authoring programs ubiquitous will push ILOs further and further in the "complex" direction. As they become more and more sophisticated, they'll require two things:

1. Heavy input from instructor-experts, whose real-world experience will be increasingly communicable through advanced ILOs and thus increasingly relevant/valuable.

2. Instructional design and development (IDD) specialists who know how to incorporate instructor-experts' knowledge into advanced ILO mechanics.

Micro-collaboration, the teaching/learning transaction that occurs between IDD specialists and instructor-experts, is important to all ILOs, and becomes increasingly indispensable as ILOs become increasingly sophisticated.

Instructor-experts /
Subject Matter Experts (SMEs)

We've chosen to use the term "instructor-expert" rather than the more common "SME" because we want to emphasize the tension between instruction and expertise inherent in the instructor-expert's position. He or she is not *only* an expert in some particular subject matter: more often than not, he or she also has some experience with *teaching* people about the subject matter, even if he or she operates in the private sector rather than academia.

Teaching experience can be a very helpful part of figuring out what ILO users need to know, but it can simultaneously incline an instructor-expert to didactic methods of pedagogy for which ILOs have little room.

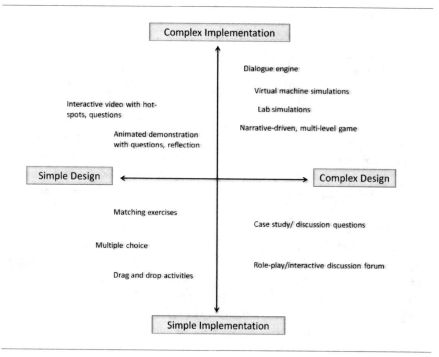

Figure 2: Graphing ILOs.

Successful micro-collaboration requires an ILO team to turn this tension between instructional habits and subject matter expertise into something productive, rather than obstructive. We don't want people to forget that there is a difference between subject matter expertise and instructional habits, and we hope the term "instructor-expert" will serve as a subtle reminder[1].

Explicit vs. Tacit Knowledge

Sophisticated ILOs impart two types of knowledge: explicit and tacit.

Instruction manuals, peer-reviewed articles, how-to videos, textbook chapters, and class- or conference-room lectures are all adequate vehicles

---

[1] For the grammatically inclined: this is also the reason for hyphenating "instructor-expert" rather than leaving it open, the idea being that its nouns have two different functions; this makes it more akin to, say, "nurse-practitioner" than "student nurse."

for explicit knowledge. It's the kind of knowledge you can pick up without an ILO (even if using an ILO might make it easier). It's exemplified by formulas, schematics, and theories, and is primarily didactic, something acquired by listening or reading and absorbing information.

Tacit knowledge is the obverse. It's the reservoir of half-conscious skills that experts acquire through years and years of *applying* their explicit knowledge. Tacit knowledge is the difference between someone who reads textbooks on the craft of painting and someone who spends hours a day in the studio, or someone who reads manuals on fly-fishing and someone who spends hours a day in the river shallows. Tacit knowledge consists of tricks of the trade, lightning-fast associations, and hard-won competencies.

Of course, if we're talking about painting or fly-fishing, then a big part of an expert's tacit knowledge will be kinesthetic, which brings us to an important point: tacit knowledge is linked to experts' *physical* occupancy of specialized spaces. One of the challenges of ILO design and development is conveying what it feels like to apply one's explicit knowledge in a professional setting. Now the vast majority of ILO projects won't have the resources to create a full virtual-reality experience. That's for astronauts and the mega-wealthy. As a result, ILOs are currently limited in their ability to replicate *tactile* learning (although even that is changing).

Therefore, instead of conveying the *physical sensation* of being in a cockpit, a call center, or a cryogenics lab, ILOs impart tacit knowledge by teaching learners to *solve problems* the way an expert would. They get learners to build the patterns of thought, or cognitive structures, that come with *using* knowledge in addition to accumulating it.

It is only possible for ILOs to do this when IDD specialists—e.g., the software developers, instructional designers, project managers, and graphic artists who all have experience with online learning—micro-collaborate with an instructor-expert. The team must work together to express the particulars of the content domain using the mechanics of online media such that end users develop expert-level cognitive habits. This is no mean feat, to say the least. And it should clarify why more advanced ILOs require more thorough micro-collaboration: the more tacit knowledge an ILO can convey, the more important it will be to accurately and comprehensively represent the experiences of real-world experts. The greater the sophistication, the higher the stakes. The higher the stakes, the more imperative it is to micro-collaborate well.

Aleckson's Five Factors

Having established our terminology and starting premises, we can now take a more detailed look at what each of the following chapters will discuss.

Chapter 1: On the Genealogy of the Five Factors. The five-factor model builds off the models of other organizational theorists, most notably Bolman and Deal (who work in partnership) and Bacharach. The former focus on organizations, the latter focuses on projects, and we focus on individuals within a project team. Whereas Bolman and Deal and Bacharach take a general view of organization/project dynamics, we address online learning in particular. We incorporate structures from both models; understanding how we've adapted them will help readers use our strategies most effectively.

Chapter 2: The More Interactivity, the Better. The interactive aspects of ILOs are what set them apart from other pedagogical instruments. To illustrate this, we'll look at a case study from academia (see "The Engage program and Cool-It" below). Of particular interest are the *design mechanics* by which online learning is made to be interactive. These mechanics are visible in commercial video games, which, even though they're not meant to be educational in the usual sense of the word, have a lot to teach us about the ways people learn.

Chapter 3: Politics: Flattening Power Relationships. The political factor deals with *enabling* micro-collaboration: micro-collaboration can be either facilitated or hindered by cultural factors on both the project and program/department levels. In order to micro-collaborate effectively, individual team members and upper-level management need to invest in a culture of egalitarianism. To put it plainly, the team's IDD specialists need to be on a level playing field with the instructor-expert, which tends to be easier said than done. IDD specialists can take the lead in leveling the playing field by implementing our communication / professional development strategies.

Chapter 4: Structure: Project Management and the Development Process. The structural factor deals with *facilitating* micro-collaboration. ILO teams don't have unlimited resources to draw on; in order to generate a high-quality end product, or deliverable, they need to use their time, personnel, and money as efficiently as possible. The best way to ensure such efficiency is to assign a dedicated project manager whose sole responsibility is monitoring the triple constraint: schedule, scope, and costs. Part of monitoring the triple constraint is establishing the process by which the ILO will go from the planning stage to its first release. ILO projects are best suited to iterative processes (e.g., Agile). Iterative development promotes formative evaluation and learning in action (both of which make ILOs better), but it requires strong project management in order to yield results.

Chapter 5: Culture: Creating a Shared Language for Micro-Collaborative Communication. The cultural factor deals with *synchronizing* the efforts of micro-collaborators. If the ILO is to be infused with the instructor-expert's tacit knowledge, then the IDD specialists must *understand* that knowledge. At the same time, the instructor-expert must understand the medium by which his or her tacit knowledge will be expressed. It's crucial for all team members to communicate their perspectives to one another; to do so, they need a shared language, a set of reference points that keeps them on the same page. Using certain documents and exercises during meetings can help establish this language, as can reference to theoretical texts on eLearning.

Chapter 6: Performance: Formative Evaluation. The performance factor deals with *interpreting and integrating* user feedback during micro-collaboration. Using formative evaluation—obtaining user feedback at various stages of the development process—makes it more likely that an ILO will achieve its educational goals. Therefore, formative evaluation is one of the most significant aspects of iterative development. It will be good for an ILO even if it is conducted informally, but teams can make the most of formative evaluation when they *formalize* it. Formal formative evaluation demands input from all team members (including the instructor-expert) and ensures that every iteration of the deliverable is a step closer to the team's long-term vision of success.

Chapter 7: Momentum: The Panoramic Factor. The momentum factor deals with *sustaining* micro-collaboration. In our model, momentum has two characteristics: it is instantiated within the other four factors, relying on them for its shape, and it also affects them all at once, such that dips in momentum cause problems all across the board. Following our strategies for success in the other four factors will lead to positive momentum, but it is also important to be aware of momentum as a separate—if somewhat unusual—factor, something that can be consciously managed and given a jolt when necessary.

The Engage Program and Cool-It

In the interest of relating our arguments to specific real-world experiences, we will spend a lot of time talking about a particular ILO called Cool-It. Cool-It was created under the auspices of the University of Wisconsin-Madison's Department of Academic Technology. Within that department is the Engage program, which "partner[s] with instructors to transform higher education by exploring, evaluating, and disseminating best practices for teaching and learning with technology" (University of Wisconsin-Madison 2011a). Engage houses multiple ILO development initiatives; Jon Aleckson's research on Engage convinced him that the program as a whole, and Cool-It in particular, were excellent examples of how good ILOs come into being.

Therefore, we will make repeated reference to Cool-It, and are deeply grateful to all the people who worked on it—both those who are named in the coming chapters and those who, for our purposes, labored behind the scenes. Their contributions have been invaluable, as our readers will doubtless agree.

Micro-Collaboration in Practice

In addition to the Cool-It case study, we've supplemented chapters 2 through 7 with brief stories from the field. These are drawn from our own professional histories or from our colleagues', and fall under the heading "Micro-Collaboration in Practice." Their purpose is to reinforce a point we made earlier in this introduction: this is a book of practical strategies based on experience. It will be obvious that these stories are only snapshots and cannot possibly do justice to every aspect of ILO development, or even every suggestion we make in a given chapter. But they will help to humanize our argument and make it easier to see how our strategies for micro-collaborative success are applicable to many different types of ILO projects.

Online Appendix

In the course of our discussion we'll make many references to things like "articulation documents" and "design blueprints." It can be helpful to have templates for such items, so we've compiled a collection of ILO development resources at www.mindmeldbook.com. There you'll find sample design timetables, meeting guidelines, game-mechanic frameworks, concept approval forms, and so on. We've put them together for your convenience; they should make it easier to start implementing our strategies for micro-collaboration.

Overview

This book is something of a crossover. It marshals support from theoretical texts but doesn't fall neatly into an academic genre. It lays out some principles of instructional design but presents them as one part of a larger picture. It deals with leadership strategies but applies to people who aren't officially in leadership positions. It's relevant to universities, corporations, non-profits, and associations alike. It's not a treatise so much as a guide to making the most of the complex and dynamic process of online-learning development.

The end users of ILOs are not our main audience, but it is they who stand to benefit most from the five factors. This is because the strategies laid out in the following chapters have a single overarching goal: to make online education more effective and, ultimately, more rewarding. To make online education more reflective of instructor-experts' actual experiences by communicating both explicit *and* tacit knowledge.

We cannot effortlessly transfer knowledge from one person to another: this isn't Star Trek®[2], and none of us can perform Spock's mind-meld trick. But because of their increasing capacity for immersive interaction, ILOs offer us the next best thing. Such is the spirit in which we're writing: we want to see all ILOs fulfill online education's great potential, because well-designed ILOs create incredible opportunities for learners.

---

[2] This book is not affiliated with *Star Trek* in any way. Unfortunately.

CHAPTER 1

On the Genealogy
of the Five Factors

Our focus is on small teams, which means we're going to spend a lot of time talking about people. About how people do their best work.

We'll start by discussing abstractions, which ought to give us pause. People have a way of defying abstractions. They have an inexhaustible capacity for making all abstract theories of interaction, even the most intellectually imposing and aesthetically advanced, look facile or frivolous. That's because people are strange; people are surprising. No model can account for their vagaries—and thank goodness for that. What makes the teaching-learning transaction so endlessly fascinating is the challenge of people's idiosyncrasies.

With that in mind, we won't pretend to have the *only* perspective on how small teams work; our model is more humble than that, and perhaps more relatable. It is based largely on decades of experience in educational technology: decades of seeing, over and over, what *usually* works and what *usually* doesn't.

We have taken that experience and turned it into a heuristic, a framework that builds on the findings of other organizational theorists while being particularly applicable to online education, and even more particularly applicable to ILO development. This framework parses the nuances of interpersonal dynamics into a set of five discrete factors, as noted in the introduction:

1. Flat power relationships (Politics)

2. Effective management (Structure)

3. Shared language (Culture)

4. Formative evaluation (Performance)

5. Momentum (All)

Such division necessitates simplification, but has the benefit of making interpersonal dynamics easier to conceptualize and easier to influence (on both the department and project level). The purpose of creating a divided framework is to provide ILO teams with a helpful tool for remembering and implementing certain behaviors, behaviors typically correlated with success. We won't insult our readers by *guaranteeing* that our model will lead to success—there's nothing more suspicious than that sort of guarantee. What we *will* do is draw on personal experience to share certain strategies that make success more *likely*.

Since those strategies didn't come into being *ex nihilo*, we'll use this chapter to trace the lineage of our model, indicating its relation to antecedent models and placing it in the larger context of organizational theory. This should help to explain the arrangement of the chapters that follow and the manner in which they all come together in the end.

Bolman and Deal

A book that expresses organizational dynamics (and management practices) as discrete but related components, as ours does, is likely indebted to Lee G. Bolman and Terrence E. Deal, authors of the seminal *Reframing Organizations: Artistry, Choice, and Leadership* (2008, 1st ed. 1991). Bolman and Deal "introduce four distinct frames—structural, human resource, political, and symbolic—each logical and powerful in its own right. Together, they help us decipher the full array of significant clues [as to how organizations function], capturing a more comprehensive picture of what's going on and what to do" (2008). For Bolman and Deal, "frames" are *interpretive strategies*. In order to understand how organizations work, we must be in command of multiple strategies, because any one strategy will clarify some problems while obscuring others.

Moreover, complete understanding of an organization requires us to not only analyze it using separate frames, but take what we've learned from each frame and *integrate* it into a coherent whole. Breaking an organization into quadrants is only useful as the first step of a process that ends not in analysis, but *synthesis*. If we do not synthesize them, and instead use them in isolation from one another, Bolman and Deal's frames act less like frames than lenses: each distorts our view of the organization in a particular way, revealing some things but hiding others. It is this mistake, the privileging of one or two frames over the rest, that leads otherwise excellent managers to their downfall.

The basics of each frame are expressible metaphorically (Bolman and Deal 2008):

Structure. The organization is a factory or a complex machine. It functions according to rules, some of which apply to everyone and some of which apply only to people in certain roles. It needs to find ways to adapt to changes in technology, and sometimes it will need to completely transform the way it operates.

Human Resources. The organization is a family. It functions according to a complex economy of skills and needs, with special attention to relationships.

Political. The organization is a jungle. Either that, or an arena—part gladiatorial battle and part chess match—in which "individuals and groups compete to achieve their parochial interests in a world of conflicting viewpoints, scarce resources, and struggles for power."

Symbolic. The organization is part temple and part theater. It has a culture all its own, one in which meaning is derived from ceremonies and rituals, in which stories propel identity-formation and heroes are the wellspring of inspiration.

Again, we can learn something about an organization by looking at it through any one of the frames. But if we use one frame exclusively, then we are going to miss important facets of how the organization works, and this will lead to problems. Missed deadlines, enraged stakeholders, disgruntled or enervated employees, bureaucratic impasses: they're all symptomatic of a failure to *integrate* the frames. The exceptional utility of Bolman and Deal's system stems from its ability to identify compartmental problems while suggesting *holistic* solutions. Its purpose is to help people become better leaders.

Bacharach

The same productive tension between compartmental and holistic management is found in Samuel Bacharach's *Keep them on Your Side: Leading and Managing for Momentum* (2006). Like Bolman and Deal, Bacharach advances a four-part model; unlike Bolman and Deal's, Bacharach's model prioritizes *momentum* at the *project* level. To start, Bacharach observes that leadership is often defined in terms of "vision," a vague, possibly mystical quality that is only weakly correlated with results (2006). He proposes that instead of reserving our honors for visionary leadership, we recognize the value of *proactive* leadership, which is distinguished, in large part, by a leader's ability to create and sustain momentum:

> In recent years, there's been an almost cultist obsession with the notion of vision, giving leadership a quasi-spiritual dimension, as though leadership were the capacity to see what has not yet been seen by others ...
>
> ... Although many aspire to be visionary and may even think of themselves as visionary, the reality is that truly successful visionaries are proactive, displaying both the *political competence* to mobilize people for action and the *managerial competence* necessary to sustain momentum and keep people on their side to achieve results. (Bacharach 2006)

As part of his argument, Bacharach quadrisects momentum into the structural, performance, cultural, and political dimensions—a crosshairs, if you will. We will revisit Bacharach in chapter 7, near the end of this book, but we'll take a moment here to sketch the rudiments of his model. *Structural* momentum involves resource management, i.e., using the right tools, or "instruments of transformation," to achieve the team's goals (Bacharach 2006). "Generally," writes Bacharach, "there are two types of resources: human resources and inanimate resources" (2006). These two types need to be properly balanced and deployed.

Performance momentum involves a leader's ability to monitor team members' accomplishments and professional development, as well as the coincidence of the team's products with the project's goals.

Cultural momentum involves "those psychological attitudes, beliefs, and cognitions that enhance one's sense of motivation and identity" (Bacharach 2006).

And *Political* momentum involves knowing how to get your organization's key players on your side—and convince them to stay.

Aleckson's Five Factors

We have found, based mainly on our professional experience, that the factors conducive to micro-collaboration within ILO teams are compatible with Bacharach's dimensions—not in the particulars, necessarily, but in the abstract. Therefore, we have begun with his crosshairs and made a few significant changes.

First, we have repositioned momentum. Instead of being the substrate that each factor is meant to express, momentum is now its *own*, dynamic factor. It does not determine the significance of the other factors, although it does flow through them all. This reflects that our focus is not on momentum per se, but on micro-collaboration. Momentum may help or hinder micro-collaboration, but it is not the whole story. With reference to Bolman and Deal, we must be able to move into and out of the momentum frame, in addition to being able to connect it with all the others.

Second, whereas one strength of the prenominate models is their generalizability, our model draws its strength from specificity. Simply put, this is a book about online learning and online learning alone. We will invoke certain widely applicable principles, especially from game-design theory, but they are not our primary focus. Our experience, our education, our expertise, and our stories from the field are all related to online learning, and we will speak directly to the particular challenges and opportunities that online learning poses. Those, after all, are the challenges and opportunities that we have faced ourselves.

Finally, while Bacharach puts his emphasis on leaders, our emphasis is on learners. Our ultimate interest is in achieving educational outcomes, which itself requires team members to learn from one another. It's obvious that Bacharach, too, is interested in teams achieving their goals—as noted above, he considers getting things done to be one of the most important ways of identifying proactive leadership. But because our model is more specific, we have a more precise set of goals in mind, and a more precise idea of who will benefit from our achieving them. We keep learners (or users) at the forefront, always remembering that for learners to get anything out of an ILO, the members of the development team must learn in kind.

Here, again, is our model in graphic form (Figure 3). The preceding review of its influences should help to place it in context—should, in other words, indicate how our model is meant to be interpreted. It is an array of collaborative strategies, each of which can be understood in isolation but should be implemented in concert with the other three. It is a starting point for articulating how ILO development teams function. A starting point for identifying what's going right and what's going wrong. The bulk of this book consists in expressing each factor as concretely as possible, with much attention given to stories of how the factors play out in real life.

Overview

The various models derivable from organizational theory serve to remind us simultaneously of our limitations and our potential. Our limitations tend to be defined by the narrowness of our habitual perceptions: if we are accustomed to looking at a team in a certain way, through a certain frame, then we may not be giving ourselves the right tools for discerning problems or reaching goals. Our potential rests in our ability to recognize, critique, and exceed our habits of perception, and it is in this respect that organizational models prove most useful.

As a model, the Five Factors of Micro-Collaboration (Figure 3) lay out the conditions under which ILO teams have the highest chance of creating a deliverable that lets users *learn by doing*. They represent a merger of well-established theoretical frameworks and real-life professional experience. Thus, in their own way, they express a balance between tacit and explicit knowledge.

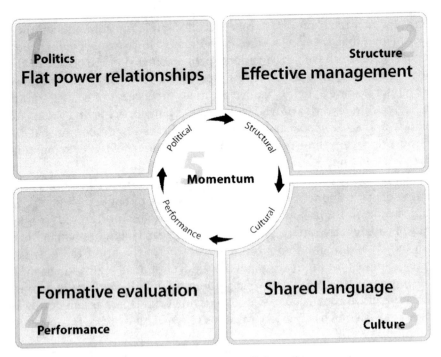

Figure 3: Aleckson's five factors of micro-collaboration.

In the next chapter, we'll begin our departure from our current, rather abstract plane of reference by discussing what it is about ILOs that makes them so useful to learners. To put it another way: what makes ILOs capable of embodying the all-important tacit/explicit balance?

CHAPTER 2

The More Interactivity, the Better

Interactivity can be viewed as a dialog between the learner and eLearning application ... The application becomes, if you will, an expert mentor with whom the learner communicates. —*Michael Allen, Michael Allen's Guide to eLearning (2003)*

In the introduction, we mentioned that all ILOs can be placed on a graph of complexity. Some are simple and less interactive, others are complex and highly interactive. To be successful, all the micro-collaborators involved with a project need to agree on where their ILO will fall on the graph. They all need to have the same vision of the end product. There may, of course, be differences in the details, but we'll discuss those in later chapters. For now, suffice it to say that detail-oriented disagreements must occur in the context of big-picture agreement. Creating any online learning activity requires asking, "What do we want this thing, the ILO, to be like when it's done? What do we want it to do for the learner? What can we afford to spend? How sophisticated should we make the artificial intelligence? How *interactive* will it be when a learner is sitting in front of it?"

In this chapter, we'll argue that more interactivity means a better experience for the learner. We'll look at the characteristics of complex ILOs and how learners respond to them. Perhaps most importantly, we'll begin our sustained examination of Cool-It, a successful ILO initiative. (As we mentioned in the introduction, Cool-It will inform the rest of the book because it illustrates micro-collaboration's real-world potential for developing rewarding, sophisticated eLearning products.) By the end, we'll have shown how putting time and effort into complex ILOs can yield big dividends for everyone involved.

The Birth of a Cryogenics ILO

Professor John Pfotenhauer, of the University of Wisconsin-Madison, was already popular with graduate students. They thought of him as a fantastic teacher. Perhaps it was his success with traditional pedagogy that motivated John to seek out new ways to impart his expertise—ways that would be available not only to more students, but also to his colleagues, both academic and corporate.

Pfotenhauer taught Mechanical Engineering Course #556 (Cryogenics) every other semester. A typical session involved him writing, explaining, and solving complex math problems on the board while his students watched and took notes. These were usually differential equations that took hours to unravel. The semester did not afford the students more than one class period for hands-on lab work.

It was, in large part, a math class. It was lecture-based, and the homework consisted mainly of solving whatever type of problem Pfotenhauer had gone over during the day. Not surprisingly, interactivity was low. Pfotenhauer began to wonder whether his students would benefit from a change in format. He had observed firsthand how interactive styles of teaching can command learners' attention:

"All our kids were home-schooled up to some point in time," Pfotenhauer says of his family. "They learned a lot by educational games, as well as through their workbooks and such. And, you know, you'd see them sitting there for four hours or eight hours, and you just can't get them away from it."

Due to his parenting experience, Pfotenhauer felt a personal attachment to the possibility of adding interactive pedagogy to his professorial tool kit. Moreover, he could see the commercial potential for an online, cryogenics-based learning object:

> I wanted to eventually create a suite of applications that would be available online for somebody out in that field and industry to learn the subject matter … Typically what will happen is, some company will develop a new product line that requires some low-temperature innovation … They point the finger at Joe and say, 'Hey, Joe, you're our new cryogenics guy.' … So I had envisioned for some time that I'd like to have some resources available online for those guys, so they could learn it, independent of a semester schedule.

Pfotenhauer applied for an Innovation Award from the Engage program, which is part of UW Madison's Department of Information Technology. When the award was granted, Engage management conferred with IT Support staff to determine who would be the best fit for Pfotenhauer's proposal, settling on project manager / instructional designer Dave Gagnon and programmer Mike Litzkow. Together, these three were the driving force behind Cool-It, an exemplary ILO of game-level sophistication.

Cool-It: The Experience

From the beginning, the stated goal of Cool-It was to allow students to assume the role of a cryogenics engineering consultant. They'd select one problem from a list of several, then go on to solve the problem by suggesting a solution according to the right procedure, the optimum order, and the ideal cost. It's a simple enough framework, but in it, the Engage team saw the potential for rich, video-game-like interactivity. Pfotenhauer, Gagnon, and Litzkow describe Cool-It gameplay in a paper presented at the 39th ASEE/IEEE Frontiers in Education Conference:

> In the first level, the cryogenic consultant encounters a set of jobs that each require him/her to select a combination of a cryogenic refrigerator (cryocooler) and a support structure so that the object of interest can be cooled to a defined steady state temperature. Both the refrigerator and the support structure are connected to the object, but while the refrigerator extracts heat from the object, the support structure, with its connection at the other end to a warm enclosure, conducts heat to the object. The consultant can choose from a set of 40 different materials for the support structure, and by adjusting sliders can change the length and cross sectional area of the structural piece(s) ... Four different cryocooler sizes can be selected, but in some cases the electric power consumed by the cooler (and proportional to its cooling capacity) is also constrained. Solutions are obtained by satisfying the strength, temperature, and electric power constraints, but the various structural material possibilities allow a wide range of associated expense, so that the set of possible solutions encompasses a wide range of system cost. Thus, while multiple satisfactory solutions may be obtained, only one will define a minimum cost to the company for whom the consultant is working ...

… One of the most valuable aspects of [the] game, both for pedagogical reasons and for the game-like feel, is the requirement to balance competing factors in order to obtain a solution." (Pfotenhauer et al. 2009, emphasis added)

The point of Cool-It is to teach learners to think as cryogenic scientists, rather than as students of cryogenic science. These are two distinct modes of processing information. To get a feel for the differences between them, the designers on the Engage team didn't just listen to Pfotenhauer talk: they actually spent time in his lab and watched him tinker. Says Gagnon, "We all wanted people to have the experience of a cryogenic engineer and get at that experience from the mad scientist point of view … You lock into the kind of learning that is not about memorizing the cost of metals, and is not about solving math problems by hand. It is about knowing the relationships between things, and forming gut reactions about what to try."

Getting learners to that point—the point at which they're seeing connections between actual objects they might find in the real world, rather than *theorizing* those connections from a *distance*, as they do when solving math problems—requires a certain degree of immersion. It requires learners to be engaged with what's happening on the screen, and, as part and parcel of that engagement, to care about whether they succeed or fail.

To increase Cool-It's verisimilitude (i.e., to encourage learners to respond to the game's challenges as if they were real-life situations, rather than abstract questions to be answered), the Engage team used narrated animations in conjunction with a video game artifice known as a "cut scene." Cut scenes function in video games to build a narrative around the player's choices, and to flesh out the characters/environments with which the player interacts.

Cut scenes can also be used to dramatize the consequences of the player's actions. In the case of Cool-It, the Engage team understood that consequences had to be a big part of the experience. Students needed to know that, in the context of the game, they could fail. Indeed, an important way of understanding the subject matter was to let students explore the consequences of failing in particular ways: Would the consequences be minor, e.g., a slight financial loss for the virtual company? Or would they be catastrophic, e.g., a submarine exploding under water? The Engage team employed a number of graphic artists and students versed in 3D modeling to imbue Cool-It's cut scenes with the desired realism.

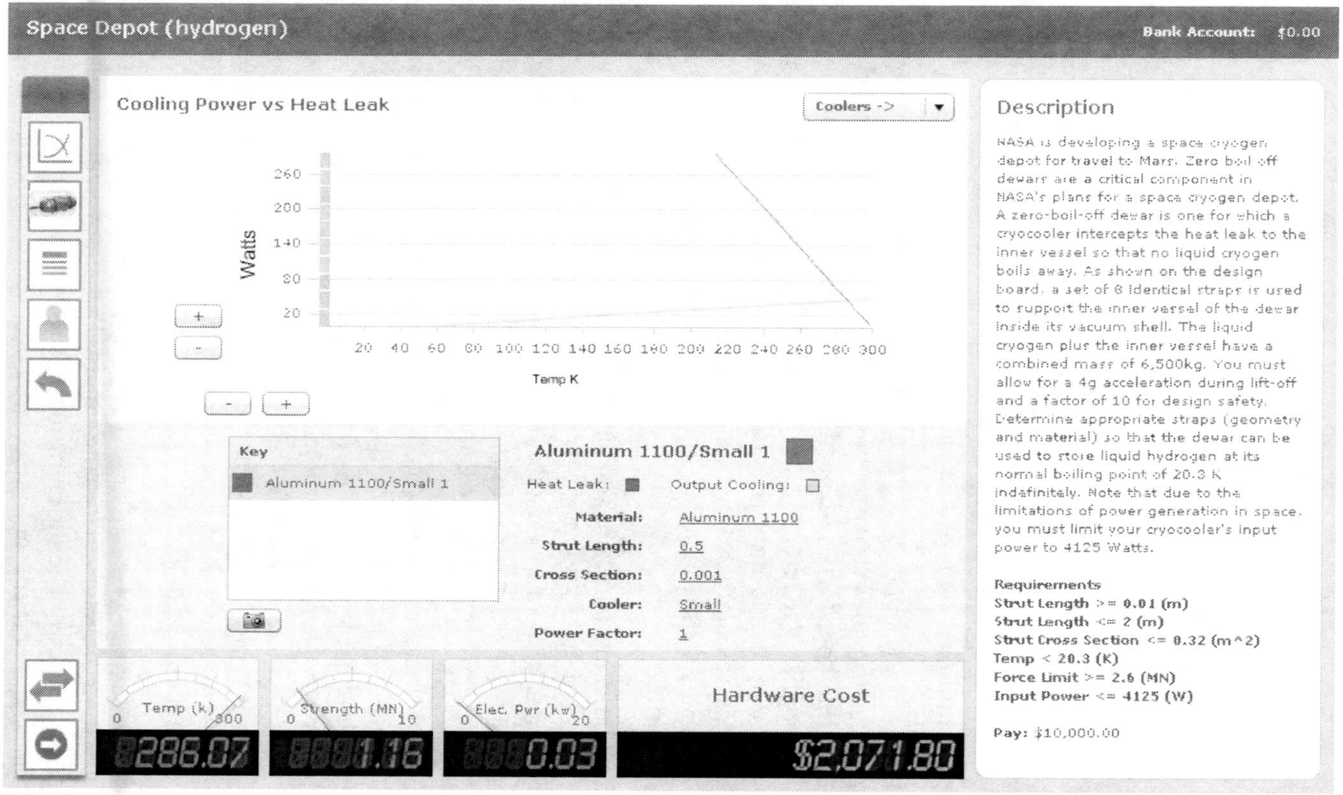

Space Depot (hydrogen)   Bank Account: $0.00

Cooling Power vs Heat Leak   Coolers -> ▶

Description

NASA is developing a space cryogen depot for travel to Mars. Zero-boil-off dewars are a critical component in NASA's plan for a space cryogen depot. A zero-boil-off dewar is one for which a cryocooler intercepts the heat leak to the inner vessel so that no liquid cryogen boils away. As shown on the design board, a set of 8 identical straps is used to support the inner vessel of the dewar inside its vacuum shell. The liquid cryogen plus the inner vessel have a combined mass of 6,500kg. You must allow for a 4g acceleration during lift-off and a factor of 10 for design safety. Determine appropriate straps (geometry and material) so that the dewar can be used to store liquid hydrogen at its normal boiling point of 20.3 K.

Note that due to the limitations of power generation in space, you must limit your cryocooler's input power to 4125 Watts.

Requirements
Strut Length >= 0.01 (m)
Strut Length <= 2 (m)
Strut Cross Section <= 0.32 (m^2)
Temp < 20.3 (K)
Force Limit >= 2.6 (MN)
Input Power <= 4125 (W)

Pay: $10,000.00

Watts

260
200
140
80
20

20 40 60 80 100 120 140 160 180 200 220 240 260 280 300
Temp K

Aluminum 1100/Small 1

Heat Leak: ■   Output Cooling: ☐
Material: Aluminum 1100
Strut Length: 0.5
Cross Section: 0.001
Cooler: Small
Power Factor: 1

Key
■ Aluminum 1100/Small 1

Temp (k) 0286.07   Strength (MN) 0084.16   Elec. Pwr (kW) 0880.03   Hardware Cost $2,071.80

Figure 4: Cool-It. © 2007-2010 The Board of Regents of the University of Wisconsin System.

This is the sort of thing that keeps learners interested. "One of the primary features of the game environment that motivated our development of Cool-It," the team wrote, "is its recognized ability to capture the attention of a player and provide an enjoyable experience through which [he or she] may explore" (Pfotenhauer et al. 2009).

The Effect of Cool-It on Learners

Of course, Cool-It is not only about creating a pleasant diversion for students. It achieves concrete pedagogical aims, as reported in the team's published findings (Pfotenhauer et al. 2009):

1. Given the opportunity to implement their classroom knowledge in an interactive setting, students are more likely to relate to that knowledge on a personal level, which makes them much more likely to retain it. It's one thing to know the properties of certain metals and the equations that describe their relationships; it's another thing to *use* that information to beat a level in a game and, thus, save the lives of innocent (virtual) submariners.

2. The game makes it possible to track students' progress in a more detailed way than traditional grading. By recording students' choices in a database and analyzing how those choices change over time, the team can assess how quickly students are getting the hang of the game's various challenges.

3. In the process of overcoming the game's challenges, students begin by thinking like novices and gradually move toward thinking like experts. By recording mouse clicks, keystrokes, time elapsed between decisions, and the sequence in which decisions are made, the team can distinguish between a player who has little experience with cryogenics and a player who knows exactly what he or she is doing. The differences, when graphed, are dramatic.

As students play the game, their decision-making operations become more and more similar to that of the expert. The game "trains the player to see the attributes of the different materials through the professional vision that would normally only be created over years of practice. [...It] introduces them to the same processes used by real-world consultants in the field of cryogenic engineering" (Pfotenhauer et al. 2009). In short, students playing Cool-It really do learn to think as *cryogenic scientists*, rather than as *students of cryogenics.*

It goes without saying that this is a huge benefit when it comes to getting the job done in real life.

As might be expected, using a game (a complex ILO, that is) as part of their coursework had a positive effect on Pfotenhauer's graduate students. To help gauge students' response to Cool-It, the Engage team used formative evaluation methods throughout the development process: they showed prototypes to groups of students and altered the game based on the students' feedback. For instance, it was students who suggested that Cool-It incorporate a level in which one could safely play around with the properties of various materials without affecting one's final score. In essence, students wanted a virtual practice room, or what's known in gaming terminology as a "tutorial level." The tutorial level is a design mechanic common to video games, and the Engage team wrote it in.

This attention to feedback paid off. Pfotenhauer recalls that after students used Cool-It, there was a "buzz of chatter" at the start of class. The game had been assigned as homework, and the questions it provoked acted as springboards for the day's lecture topic.

> All I have to say is: 'So, what did you learn?' And there's quite a bit that they learned already. Like specific materials that are the best ones. And some of them noticed that the shape of the thermal conductivity current was different for the different materials. *Perfect* ... And, you know, it just launched us into the topic about thermal conductivity at low temperatures, which is what I would cover anyway in a lecture. But now, it's interactive, because they've seen it and they've got comments, and they've got questions, [because they've experienced the feeling of tinkering.]

Students came to class with their own sense of investment in the lecture topic. They knew what it would mean to use the day's lesson in a real-life, potentially high-stakes situation, and they wanted to get it right.

Video Games and ILOs:
How Entertainment Creates Interaction

Video games—their architecture, their features, the experience they offer their end users—exerted a substantial influence on Cool-It. There's a certain irony in this: after all, video games are notorious for distracting students from their schoolwork and rotting their impressionable brains. For years, video games have played the part of the villain in a grim apocalyptic battle with our noble teachers; according to this popular schema, video games are stupefying, narcotizing, and possibly to blame for the erosion of free society.

In the case of certain games, that assessment *may* be fair. There are lots of video games out there. Some of them are awful—but then, some are masterful in their own way. Indeed, academics these days realize that video games and simulations have inherent characteristics that, if successfully developed and deployed, can be potent pedagogical tools that will enhance even the simplest learning activity.

"I see engaging the learner...as giving [him or her] a series of achievable challenges," says William Horton, author of *eLearning by Design* (2006). "If a learner encounters a well-placed difficulty within the online learning [object] and [he or she] works to solve it, it becomes incredibly satisfying and sometimes fun. That's why I think video games are so addictive and our learning objects need [to] be too."

The very abundance of video games means that they need to be highly effective at teaching players *how* they should be played. James Paul Gee, author of *What Video Games Have to Teach us about Learning and Literacy* (2003), observes that if a game is a poor teacher, then it's likely to end up on the scrap heap, because there are many other options from which to choose. A game has to *instruct* us as to how we move through its world, and it has to do it well. How do we tell when we can pick up an item? How do we relay orders to our army? How do we transform from a little dinosaur into a big one? How do we select a single weapon from the vast array we appear to carry? If the game doesn't do an excellent job of teaching us these basic things, then we won't have much fun with it.

Therefore, most games start with a tutorial level (like the one built into Cool-It). But, as Gee notes, learning the basics is rarely enough (2003). Many video games put players through a series of distinct challenges, each more demanding than the last. With every successive challenge, the stakes get higher and the rewards get sweeter. Players must gradually learn to solve problems of greater and greater complexity; the basic skills they start with won't be enough to carry them through to the end. If you've ever played a video game, you probably remember how impossible the first level seemed at the outset, and how laughably easy it seemed by the time you were at the final stage.

Challenge/teach, challenge/teach, over and over. That's how video games are built, and gamers respond: online, you can find thousands and thousands of documents created by players to compare notes on strategies for success. Gamers' sheer enthusiasm leads organically to group mentoring. The passion and attention to detail visible in these documents is the envy of most traditional educators.

Principles of Game-based Learning

Kurt Squire, assistant professor of Educational Communications and Technology at UW-Madison and current director of the Games, Learning and Society Initiative, notes that video games and other serious interactive objects "provide situated experiences where players are immersed in complex problem-solving tasks. Good games teach players more than just facts, and [can introduce new] ways of seeing and understanding problems, even opportunities to 'become' different kinds of people." Squire lays out seven principles[1] on which the emergent paradigm of game-based learning is built (2003):

1. Create emotionally compelling contexts for learning.

2. Situate the learner in complex information-management and decision-making situations, where facts and knowledge are accessed for the purpose of *doing*.

3. Construct challenges that both confront and build on the learner's pre-existing beliefs.

4. Construct challenges that lead to productive future understandings.

5. Anticipate the learner's experiences from moment to moment, providing a range of activities to address the learner's needs.

6. Invite the learner to participate in constructing solutions and interpretations.

7. Embrace the ideologically driven nature of education and training.

---

[1] Squire's principles reflect similar frameworks developed by adult and problem-based learning theorists (see the online appendix for expansion on this point).

Figure 5: A shot from Civilization, one of the games analyzed by UW-Madison's Kurt Squire. © 2010 Take-Two Interactive Software and its subsidiaries.

Clearly, there are overlaps between the techniques an instructor might choose for teaching in the classroom and the choices a designer makes when developing a game or simulation. Some instructors choose a heavily didactic approach; think of the archetypal, tweed-clad professor standing behind an oaken lectern. So it was with early educational games: they were drill-and-practice exercises involving math equations or vocabulary words, or multiple-choice quizzes decked out with game-show trappings (Egenfeldt-Nielsen 2006). These days, of course, educational games are far more engaging: they are more akin to the instructor who weaves questions into the lecture, requiring learners to think and respond. The instructor who is attuned to learners' interest and enthusiasm. The instructor who, rather than play the sage on the stage, plans the class period in such a way that the learners are front and center.

Game-studies researchers argue that educational games should be designed to keep learners at the edge of competency by gradually increasing in difficulty. This, too, is a technique that classroom instructors have used for a long time: they scaffold learning objectives so as to climb to ever

Figure 6. Play True Challenge. This video-game-like ILO has two worlds: sport and life. There is the casual side of the game (playing sports), which includes simple input mechanics (press the button to jump), fun graphics, and a game-level degree of responsiveness, along with strategic options and a high degree of personalization of the avatar's attributes. Performance factors are tracked and displayed via a statistics card. Then there is the adventure side of the game (life decisions), which involves fun graphics, an easy-to-navigate interface, and changes in outcomes based on (1) choices made in the storyline and (2) success or failure in the casual (sports) side. Game performance statistics are affected by decisions made on the adventure (life) side. © 2010 World Anti-Doping Agency.

more challenging goals. Video game mechanics can augment this process dramatically, because video games provide a new dimension of context, or experience. Learning and meaning-creation are often situated in experience, and video games, even as they scaffold the difficulty of their challenges, generate analogs for real-life experience: identity formation, affiliation with content or space, risk-taking, consequences attendant on choices, resource management, power fantasies, storylines, physical experimentation, and well-ordered problems involving multifarious variables (Gee 2003; Egenfeldt-Nielson 2006). A video game player must concomitantly acquire and employ new knowledge in order to succeed.

Overview

There may come a day when ILOs look and operate exactly like high-end commercial video games; i.e., those that are endorsed by celebrities and advertised during Super Bowls, like the *Call of Duty* franchise. Won't that be wonderful? Yes—but unfortunately, it remains a distant dream. Commercial video games require years and tens (sometimes hundreds) of millions of dollars to produce. A typical ILO project will be allotted a mere fraction of the resources that go into popular entertainment titles. So if you start out expecting to generate a cross between *New Scientist* and *Crysis2*, you're likely to be disappointed. Nine times out of ten, the money won't be there.

What we want ILO development teams to take from video games are the basics, the mechanics, the *structural* elements that draw players in. They don't have to be flashy—flashy has a place, but it's not everything. The point of this chapter has not been to convince you that ILOs will fail if they don't look like video games, but to identify which aspects of video games are transferable to ILOs, and why it's worth it to transfer them. How successfully you integrate video game mechanics into your ILO's design will depend, in large part, on how *efficiently* your team deploys its resources—in other words, how well you balance the five factors. A crucial element of this efficiency is getting the instructor-expert and the IDD team to relate to one another in a productive way; that's what we'll examine in the next chapter.

<<MICRO-COLLABORATION IN PRACTICE>>

By Penny Ralston-Berg with Amy Dietz
The Collective Bargaining ILO: Using Ingenuity to Increase
Interactivity without Increasing Cost

Penn State's World Campus offers a master's degree in human resources and employment relations (HRER) and an undergraduate degree in Labor and Employment Relations (LER). Within the HRER/LER program is a fifteen-week course—called Labor and Employment: Collective Bargaining—for which we developed an ILO. This course is a required course for the LER certificate, counts toward the requirements for the LER majors and may be used to fulfil an elective requirement (3 credits) in the HRER masters program. We didn't have the resources to rely on programming elements to increase interactivity, so we had to come up with other ways to keep the learners engaged. The ILO's purpose is to let students play the roles of management, labor union, and neutral mediator in a contract negotiation. The experience is highly interactive, and gives students the chance to apply the concepts, demonstrate the skills, and practice the strategies they learn during the first six weeks of the course. They have to collaborate, conduct topical research, synthesize information, write, make critical decisions, and, most importantly, negotiate.

The ILO plays out over five weeks, during which students work in small groups to establish a mock collective-bargaining agreement for a made-up company in Indianapolis, Indiana. Each student is assigned to a team that represents the management, labor union, or neutral mediator position. These teams all have different parts to play in weekly lessons.

From the instructions:

> Each team has the duty to bargain for the best contract for their constituency. The neutral team is responsible for presenting an *initial* proposal to the final proposal board but will also assume the role of mediator in the collective bargaining negotiations. This means that the neutral team will, after their review of the proposals submitted by

the union and management team each week, give feedback on the submitted proposals and make suggestions in
order to facilitate a collective bargaining agreement during the negotiations. Labor and management teams
should negotiate with each other, but if the neutral team
sees an issue on one side or another that may be stalling
the negotiations, they have the authority to approach the
team and make suggestions in order to keep the negotiations moving. The labor or management team is not
forced to incorporate the suggestions of the neutral team
if it conflicts with a key sticking point, but at the same
time, the team should carefully consider the neutral
team's suggestions as their task is to offer the most fair
and balanced solution based on the information available
to both sides. The instructor will expect teams to bargain
in good faith. (© Penn State World Campus. Reprinted
with permission.)

During the first two weeks, students draft an overall proposal that
identifies the key bargaining issues each team will address. They use a
mock negotiation problem between the Auto Products Corporation and
the Local 5000 (United Metal Workers of America) as a starting point.
Each team conducts research about the area to learn more about its con-
stituents, form its arguments, and present its case.

In the third week, teams (management or union) develop proposals
related to wages. In the fourth week, they develop proposals related to
benefits. In the fifth and final week, they develop proposals related to job
security and seniority, and submit proposals for negotiation.

Transparency and Verisimilitude

One of the responsibilities of the IDD team is to make sure that the technology involved in the ILO doesn't short-circuit the learning activity.

"The original discussion exercise was on the same board and there
was no privacy between groups," says Amy Dietz, a lecturer in Penn
State's Labor Studies and Employment Relations department and admin-
istrator of the online HRER program. "Everyone could see the other
groups' posts. I could not understand this since if you are trying to negotiate you need privacy. So we created different boards for the different

groups and the main board for the main negotiation. Then we found out that we needed activities each week that we could grade."

From the instructions:

> Interaction takes place on two levels:
>
> In the team discussions members share research, collaborate in proposal development and strategy development, problem solving, preparing/assisting designated spokesperson(s) for negotiations, etc. A private team discussion board is provided to discuss strategy and position.
>
> In negotiation discussions a designated spokesperson or spokespersons from each team will be representing their team during the negotiations following the submission of the proposal. Team members are actively involved with assisting spokesperson(s) as needed. Each side trades counter proposals with the other teams and continues to negotiate on the proposal/negotiation discussion forum. (© Penn State World Campus. Reprinted with permission.)

During a recent course revision, we considered incorporating *Second Life* into virtual negotiations. The idea was to let students meet in real time around a negotiation table; they could design avatars that looked right for each role, complete with characteristic gestures and facial expressions. However, we found that the learning curve for using *Second Life*, combined with the scheduling difficulties that come with students living in different time zones, meant that the logistical challenges associated with using *Second Life* outweighed the increased educational value.

Grading in Increments

Higher-education courses often stretch simulations out over several weeks to accommodate the standard fifteen-week format. Given this extended time period, individual pieces of the ILO can be broken into smaller, graded assignments, which gives students more time to collaborate, reflect, revise, and hone their negotiation skills. Moreover, grading in increments helps keep adult learners on task. Most students in HRER's online program have many obligations outside of school, including full-time jobs. Given the many priorities competing for adult learners' at-

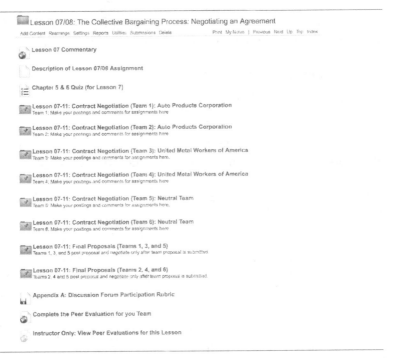

Figure 7. The faculty view of the student teams' discussion boards. In higher education, online course offerings are presented in a CMS or LMS package; each discussion board can be seen as an opportunity for an ILO. Even in a relatively simple format such as this, video game mechanics can improve learners' experiences. (© Penn State World Campus. Reprinted with permission.)

tention, projects with a deadline off in the distance tend to be relegated to the back burner until they're due—or nearly due. That would be a serious problem in the case of the collective bargaining simulation, which requires a great deal of research and response and can't possibly be completed in an eleventh-hour rush. Using deadlines to break this large project into smaller units of work helps avoid that scenario. It sets a manageable pace and keeps the project at or near the forefront of students' efforts.

Finally, grading in increments helps maintain accountability during the simulation and gives students a chance to improve their work with every week. At the end of each week, students are asked to rate one another's contributions using a peer review form; they're held accountable for how much they help the team, and receive suggestions as to how they can improve. These peer reviews come into consideration when students' grades are calculated.

Simulation and Work Experience

The collective bargaining ILO has been revised and refined over time based on instructor experience and student feedback. Immediately after the activity, students have the opportunity to share their thoughts about what went right, what went wrong, and how things could be improved.

On the whole, the evaluations indicate that students are passionate about their teams. They tend to become emotionally involved in the simulation's outcome. According to Dietz,

> [The collective bargaining students are mostly] toward the end of their academic experience, and they are pretty savvy online learners. What I really like about these courses is the discussions, the group work. This is probably the most challenging part of it, but it is also where students get fired up and get pretty engaged.

> Usually I get feedback that students think [the collective bargaining simulation] should be worth a bigger part of their course grade, even though it is already thirty percent. The simulation goes on weeks, and they put in a ton of work.

They love it at the end because they find they learn so much about the process that they can translate into their work experience. Even though many may never be involved in collective bargaining, there is a lot to be learned about just interpersonal relationships."

CHAPTER 3

Politics: Flattening Power Relationships

Collaboration is "co-laboring" with others to achieve a
common goal. The only nuance is that the relationship is
characterized by an absence of positional or formal
authority on the part of the participating individuals. In
other words, people who are co-laboring influence others
in the group through their personal power (expertise,
information, and experiences). — *Les Howles, Project
Manager, UW Engage Program*

If they're going to micro-collaborate on an ILO, the IDD team and the instructor-expert need to meet on equal footing. This is easier said than
done; any effort at micro-collaboration will call for creativity and flexibility
at both the project and program levels. As part of an ILO development
team, you'll be in position to make a much bigger difference on the project
level. Even so, we'll be talking about both strata, because program- or department-level policies impact how project teams function. The more you
know about *everyone's* role, the better you'll be at assessing your own role
and finding innovative solutions to roadblocks.

Old Habits and the Culture that Reinforces Them

In the university setting, there was a time when the Department of In-
structional/Informational Technology Support (in this chapter, we'll call
it "IT") existed mainly to help professors get their projectors running and
their microphones plugged in; later, it was on call to get computers and
software booted up. Those days are long gone, but sometimes, IT staff are
still treated as if they hadn't evolved—as if they were still A/V "support

49

geeks." A similar problem is present in the business world, where highly sought-after instructor-experts often see IDD work as cabalistic and tangential to the business's mission.

Obviously, today's IDD teams bring much more to the table than the ability to distinguish between input and output jacks. If they didn't, this book wouldn't need to exist.

Now let us pause for a moment to say, very clearly and very early, that we are not out to minimize the role of instructor-experts: there's no question that instructor-experts' knowledge and experience are invaluable. If that weren't true, we wouldn't worry about their level of involvement. The concept of ILOs is *predicated* on the importance of what instructor-experts have to offer. That importance can't be overstated. Unfortunately, it's prone to overshadowing the IDD team's importance. Therein lies the issue.

If the instructor-expert is the *only* team member whose knowledge and experience are recognized, then any effort at micro-collaboration is going to founder. Why? In short, because we're talking about human beings, and human beings need to be respected in order to do good work. When the IDD team feels it's being treated unfairly—i.e., as unequivocally subordinate to the instructor-expert, rather than as an integral part of a collaboration—the ILO is going to suffer. A dismissive or domineering instructor-expert will provoke a sour attitude, a draining of passion, a chorus of "why should we care?"—even if he or she doesn't mean to. The IDD team will end up frustrated, the instructor-expert will end up frustrated, and the ILO will end up lackluster.

Of course, most instructor-experts won't react quite so poorly to the IDD team, but it does happen, especially in university cultures. We've come across instructor-experts who see instructional designers as being there to add "bells and whistles" to their courses. Much of the time, instructor-experts don't even realize that this is a dismissive attitude. But it has serious ramifications. IDD teams often have multiple projects to work on, and they'll be inclined to devote their efforts to projects in which their relationship with the instructor-expert is more micro-collaborative. The project of the dismissive instructor-expert will get as little attention as the instructor-expert expects.

Other instructor-experts are not so much dismissive as resistant, even obstructive. In the case of an instructor-expert with an autocratic style of communication, the design team can end up feeling offended, which leads to nothing good.

If you're an instructor-expert, the message is simple: afford the IDD team the same respect you'd afford to colleagues in your field. You might already do so; if not, consider re-examining your habits. Just reading this book is a start. Knowing what the IDD team is going through will help you to make constructive suggestions without alienating anyone.

Professional Development and Perceived Expertise

Our personal strategies for flattening power relationships focus on the IDD team members. This is because instructor-experts are already treated as highly skilled professionals; we don't want to change that. Instructor-experts *are* professionals, and they deserve to be treated accordingly. Our point is that IDD team members are *also* professionals, and working on an ILO initiative gives them an excellent chance to prove it. Designers micro-collaborating on an ILO need to hold themselves to high standards of professionalism and expertise, and, when called for, need to be able to *convince* instructor-experts to change their deep-seated behaviors. As Les Howles (of the Engage program) put it, "You don't have formal authority ... you need to use influencing skills ... and your biggest influence is perceived expertise."

To this end, IDD team members need to redefine their traditional skill set. They're already experts in design and development; that goes without saying. But when it comes to micro-collaboration, they must also be experts in the more theoretical area of how software development relates to pedagogy. Thus, working on ILO initiatives is an excellent opportunity for IDD team members to pursue professional development. By concentrating on the following professional-development goals, they can dramatically increase the chances of a successful micro-collaboration:

1. Be conversant with academic studies of how well-designed ILOs can advance pedagogical aims and solve pedagogical problems. A designer should be making suggestions based not only how the technology works, but on how potential learners will *respond* to the technology. (Some good texts to start with are Kurt Squire's *Video Games and Learning: Teaching and Participatory Culture in the Digital Age*, William Horton's *eLearning by Design*, George Piskurich's *Rapid Instructional Design*, and Clark Aldrich's *Simulations and the Future of Learning*; see the online appendix for more.)

2. Participate in professional organizations. Keep up with new literature in the field (just as would any tenured faculty member) by reading journals and applied writings like Learning Solutions Magazine, and TechTrends (again, you can find more suggestions in the online appendix). Attend at least one conference per year: Sloan, USDLA, UW Distance Teaching and Learning, or the eLearning Guild's online PD sessions. Certificates and advanced degrees in IDD-related fields (including degrees from online universities) can go a long way toward amplifying professional credibility.

3. Cultivate the ability to *articulate* how ILOs can meet the needs of instructor-experts, even to people who know next to nothing about software design. Use case studies of past projects and portfolios of successful outcomes as examples—these bring the conversation out of the abstract and into the particular. Instructor-experts tend to gain a lot of enthusiasm for an ILO project when they feel they're *learning* about what the IDD team does, and no longer feel the need to dictate what the IDD team *should* do.

4. Ensure that design and development unfold according to a set *process*, rather than haphazardly. This process should be visible to everyone on the team; everyone should be able to agree on it, and everyone should know his or her role. (In chapter 4, we'll discuss this in much greater detail.)

5. Agree from the outset that your mission is to create a powerful learning experience for the ILO's users; to this end, set benchmark goals by looking at successful ILOs.

6. Demonstrate the tools of your profession: inform the instructor-expert of *what* you're doing and *how* you're doing it, rather than simply presenting him or her with a finished product. (You can do this through the use of brainstorming techniques, visual representation techniques, and the KJ method of reflecting on user feedback, all of which will come up again in chapter 5.)

7. Engage in traditional scholarship with regard to technology, games, distance learning, instructional design, etc. Publish articles. Present at conferences. Ask instructor-experts to co-

author or co-present, and work with them to find more opportunities for research.

The Art of Persuasion

Adhering to the above professional-development commitments will give members of the IDD team the right to expect the instructor-expert to treat them as colleagues, rather than minions. But a right is not a guarantee—some instructor-experts, their habits having been reinforced over the course of many years, will need to be brought around. In this regard, subtlety works better than blunt demands.

The following strategies can be useful when working with dismissive instructor-experts—all of them are related to the professional development goals listed above:

1. Create an overall design plan for the class. Separate the technology from the plan, for the moment. Work with the instructor-expert to determine course topics, flow, learning events, and objectives. This shows that you care about the course as a whole, not just the parts centered on technology.

2. When answering questions about technology, also include your assessment of the instructional value of the technology, and the pros and cons of using the technology for instruction. This demonstrates that you're looking for the best way to integrate the technology to enhance student learning.

3. Provide feedback on content and activities from the student point of view. Rather than telling an instructor-expert that his or her questions are confusing, ask, "From a student's perspective, I would do this…is that what you had planned for this activity?" That way, you're offering constructive criticism without creating a "my way or your way" situation.

When working with an autocratic instructor-expert, it's important to remember that the primary reason instructor-experts argue with design decisions is that they're passionate about their courses. They care. They've had autonomous control over their courses for some time, and trust isn't going to come instantaneously—you have to build it up. It can be frustrating, but keep in mind that it's much worse to have an instructor-expert who *doesn't* care about the course, who isn't willing to argue, debate, or discuss any ideas to find good solutions for learners.

Apathetic instructor experts are less common than instructor-experts who fear the usurpation of their roles and the distortion of their ideas. Indeed, researchers have found that "lack of know-how, loss of control, and loss of privacy are grounds for educators' reluctance to embrace ... new [teaching technology] systems ... and require greater attention to those feelings" (Duning et al. 1993). This means that for the IDD team, it's necessary to make the prospect of the ILO less threatening—that is, to help the instructor-expert *own* the technology in a personal way.

We have three methods of winning over impassioned, sometimes insecure instructor-experts:

1. Emphasize that you're on the same side: You, too, care about the course. You, too, want students to have a good learning experience. You don't want the instructor-expert to commit to anything that makes him or her uncomfortable.

2. Accept relinquishing some power—conditionally. Give the instructor-expert final approval of any idea. That eventually ends up giving you *more* influence over the project, because the instructor-expert has an easier time trusting you, and you start working together on a more even level. By being careful to frame your ideas as *options* and *suggestions*, you're able to establish a much more productive collaboration.

3. Reassure the instructor-expert that not everything needs to happen at once. The change from face-to-face teaching to using ILOs can be jarring and somewhat overwhelming, and rushing won't help. The important thing is to provide a solid instructional foundation and positive learning experience for students. Enhancements and additional ILOs can be added over time based on student feedback. Ideas can be tabled for future versions of the course. This shows respect for the instructor-expert's comfort level and skill set.

Mutuality and Professionalism

Along the same lines, William Horton (a corporate eLearning designer and visionary) avers, "you have to give respect to get respect." Designing ILOs is not the instructor-expert's full-time job; as a member of the IDD team, you'll need to emphasize what you can do for the instructor-expert. How can you meet his or her particular needs? Why will micro-collaboration be worth the instructor-expert's while?

During one eLearning project, Horton demonstrated his quid pro quo mentality by volunteering to write and format a white paper with the instructor-expert. This provided a forum in which the instructor-expert could include heavy-duty mathematical formulas that were out of place in the ILO, and bonded the ILO team over a project that was small in scale but high on the instructor-expert's list of priorities.

In addition, writing the white paper resulted in Horton's becoming immersed in the content domain. According to him, eLearning designers need to be well-versed in the instructor-expert's field; at the very least, they should study the subject enough to demonstrate a passion for it. Says Horton, "I come to the early meetings with the expert's textbooks and journal articles, and I try to ask a sophisticated question to show them I am not going to waste their time asking questions I could have answered by reading their work or other sources on the subject. At the very least, [you should] know the vocabulary and use it in early meetings with the expert." Getting a grip on the instructor-expert's lexicon will go a long way toward establishing that crucial level of trust on which micro-collaboration hinges.

We have, however, observed that this strategy can backfire. Even as you educate yourself in the basics of the instructor-expert's field, remember that from his or her standpoint, you're still a beginner—just as he or she is probably a beginner when it comes to software design and development. Your goal in picking up parts of the instructor-expert's lexicon is not to assert yourself as an authority by leaning on introductory texts. That will come across as arrogant. Rather, your goal is to demonstrate a willingness to learn. You are not there to teach the instructor-expert about his or her field; you are there to *absorb* and *convey* the instructor-expert's *tacit knowledge*. You can demonstrate this in conversation by first listening to the instructor-expert, then summarizing what he or she just told you. This shows that you're paying attention and are capable of understanding and synthesizing specific content without distorting it. And if you're getting the message wrong, it will serve as a solid indication that learners might also get it wrong.

Professors and Industry Experts

Horton, of course, knows that there are different types of professors. Some tend to encourage interactivity in the classroom: they monitor eye contact, they solicit responses, they block out time for hands-on activities. Others take a more traditionally didactic approach: they lecture to a quiet audience for the allotted time, then take their leave. Industry experts—

that is, instructor-experts working in the business sphere, rather than the academic—tend to resemble these latter, traditionally didactic professors.

Whether the instructor-expert is in business or academe, it's almost invariably futile for the IDD team to try to change his or her teaching habits. Instead, the IDD team should focus on convincing the instructor-expert that the ILO can and should be different. It is not meant to replicate the experience of a lecture. In part, this means establishing that the IDD team, being composed of professionals, will make the ILO project as painless as possible. It also means that no one on the IDD team will deliver monologues to the instructor-expert that draw lines in the sand: "This is your role, stay over there, this is our role, we'll stay over here." Rather, to craft a complex ILO out of didactic lecture material, the IDD team must:

1. Find ways to show their respect for what the instructor-expert does.

2. Do something for the instructor-expert that gets him or her enthusiastic about the project. Brainstorm ways to make him or her look good.

3. Demonstrate passion for the domain area by doing advance reading and picking up some of the instructor-expert's specialized vocabulary.

4. Understand how the subject domain appears to a novice, and conduct user testing in the analysis stage.

5. Focus on what really needs to be imparted to learners.

6. Get the instructor-expert to view each learning objective as a problem that the team will solve together.

7. Discuss the success of video games as teaching tools, and why learning by doing, even in a virtual setting, is important.

Talking about Video Games

That last point, the success of video games as teaching tools, warrants some expansion. Discussing the mechanics of video games—e.g., problem-driven experiences, game-based practice, graduated levels of difficulty, narrative context, and consequences for failure—is a way for the IDD team and instructor-expert to pin down exactly how much the ILO should have in common with a commercial video game, and why. The IDD team could, for instance, bring up the work of MIT's Games-to-Teach group, which created fifteen conceptual frameworks for educational games. Kurt Squire notes that once everyone involved with the project can express an informed opinion on the basic design elements of video games, those elements will play the role of shooting and editing rules for film makers: a syntax that facilitates discussion amongst members of the production team (2003).

Even when it comes to simple ILOs, the project team can make use of video game elements by:

1. Writing a storyline surrounding the course's learning objectives (as with Cool-It, in which the cryogenics scientist had to keep the submarine from exploding).

2. Creating a character that fits into the storyline, someone with whom the learner can identify.

Figure 8. You might be surprised at the number of bartenders who have no beer-pouring skill. This video-game-like training program contains "Score Your Pour" mini-game that conveys the tactile understanding of proper angle and distance required to pour the perfect glass of beer. © 2006 Miller Brewing.

3. Establishing goals that the learner must accomplish in order to advance to the next level.

4. Elaborating a context in which the learner's character suffers consequences for making the wrong choice and is rewarded for making the right one.

5. Using specific, concrete problems, such as would be found in a real-world situation, as opposed to mathematical equations or abstract engineering questions.

6. Providing game-based reasons for the learner to listen to a lecture or read a journal—e.g., information found in the journal is crucial to opening the gateway to the ILO's next stage.

The Other Side of the Coin: Advice for Instructor-experts

As we said, our strategies have focused on *convincing* instructor-experts to change old habits not because IDD people are perfect, but because instructor-experts usually don't have to prove anything. For the most part, they're seen as professionals by default. There will come projects, however, in which highly skilled and dedicated instructor-experts end up working with novice, overtaxed, or reluctant IDD specialists. If you're an instructor-expert in that situation, what do you do?

1. Share your passion. Tell stories about why this course or ILO is important to you.

2. Keep in touch with the designers on a regular basis, and if you can't get a fair share of their time, raise a flag to management sooner rather than later.

3. Remember that designers can't be expected to know everything about the subject matter from day one: they'll need time to learn, and you can help them with that.

4. Solicit ideas for new technological elements; for instance, "Do we have the capacity to do branching dialogue?"

5. Ask for another perspective: if you were a student in this online course, how would you approach a particular activity? Would you have any questions prior to getting started?

6. Talk over the objectives for the course and for each teaching module.

7. Seek out opinions and ideas for interactive activities that specifically relate to the learning objectives.

8. Demonstrate your experience. Have you worked on ILOs before? Can you show them to your designer? Are there elements from other ILOs that can be repurposed for the current project?

9. Ask, plain and simple, "How can I help? What kind of information can I provide to move the process in the right direction, and what form do you need it in?"

10. Ask IDD team members what type of tools they use to help communicate ideas. Consider asking management for experienced IDD team members and only work with "work-study students" who are mentioned by professionals.

Collaboration within the Cool-It Team

Cool-It was developed by an exceptionally compatible cadre, the core of which consisted of Dave Gagnon (the project manager / instructional designer), John Pfotenhauer (the instructor-expert), and Mike Litzkow (the programmer). Allow us to repeat: we've placed so much of our focus on this team because it serves to exemplify the power of micro-collaboration. When people work well together, blending expertise and mutual respect, they can accomplish quite a lot. Even if certain things don't go as planned (as we'll see in chapter 4).

To get a sense of how the Cool-It team interacted, it's enough to look at how they talked about one another in interviews. Litzkow, the programmer, was so impressed with the group's collective attitude and accomplishments that he defined collaboration as being "all about the personality mesh of the team, period." In this respect, Litzkow considered Gagnon the "glue" that held the team together.

Gagnon, the project manager / instructional designer, referred to Litzkow as "brilliant in ten different directions at once." Litzkow was tapped for Cool-It partly because he had experience in faculty technology-support, and was ready to move beyond the traditional work-for-hire setup. "Academic Technology is [typically] a job shop," he said. "They get paid to do it. When a client says do something, you do it. You don't tell the client, even diplomatically, 'This is a dumb idea.'" Litzkow's experiences had obviously inclined him to seek out micro-collaborative environments: "It is important to start off early with the idea that this is teamwork. It takes people with diverse talents to put together a good game [that is, ILO]. The [instructor-expert] is essential, but they are not in charge. They need to look at other individuals as on a level playing field."

He was right, and Pfotenhauer, the instructor-expert, agreed: "We have a real good balance of lots of different expertise. I have the expertise of the content, but it's very obvious that, you know, there are others, like Mike Litzkow, who has the expertise about how to make the programming happen, and the animators, to add features. And frankly, David [Gagnon] has the expertise of knowing how to make it game-like, so that it's beyond just a simulator that makes you calculate things easily."

(It's worth pausing for a moment to highlight Pfotenhauer's reference to animators: we should keep in mind that although the three team members mentioned here are most germane to our study, they were *not* the only people involved with Cool-It.)

For his part, Gagnon called Pfotenhauer "a great teacher, and someone who has good relationships with students."

The Cool-It team considered micro-collaboration a top priority, and it paid off. Their ILO met or exceeded industry standards, and their findings received national attention in the form of a published paper—jointly authored, of course.

Managers on the Program (or Organizational) Level

IT staff and instructor-experts alike will know that micro-collaboration doesn't happen in a vacuum. ILO projects tend to be undertaken by universities and corporate enterprises, both of which are almost always hierarchical. As a result, the people on the front lines of the project (the IDD team and the instructor-expert) depend on the people above them (IT department/program managers) to help make micro-collaboration possible. The wrong type of culture can make it very difficult for micro-collaboration to succeed, no matter how diligently the IDD team and instructor-expert follow our personal strategies for flattening power relationships. Those strategies will be much more effective in a context that's *conducive* to micro-collaboration. Therefore, when an organization wants to generate high-quality eLearning products, including ILOs with the sophistication of videogames, a certain onus falls on the upper levels of the hierarchy: they must create the necessary *culture* by instituting the right policies.

Just as our project-level strategies for flattening power relationships focus on the IDD team members, our program-level strategies focus on IT department/program managers—specifically, on their leadership decisions. Again, when instructor-experts understand how IT managers are nurturing micro-collaboration, it will improve the collaboration as a whole.

IT managers (at both the department and program levels) need to expect and reward the professional development of individual designers. One way of doing so is to make the IDD team's offices and website *appear* professional. Departments that foster micro-collaboration display an aesthetic of self-respect. Instead of warrens of bland cubicles arrayed beneath fluorescent panels, well-run IDD departments make use of open space, good lighting, and sophisticated décor—they look less like the stereotypical hovels of technology wonks than the vibrant workspaces of hip creative boutiques.

Along the same lines, IT management should play an active role in exposing team members to the work of academics who study the relationship between pedagogy and advanced technology. Upper management should foster an attitude of continuous improvement by setting aside time for team members to discuss what they're learning and brainstorm ways of applying it to ongoing projects. Chris Lupton, a manager of the Engage program, says,

> We train ourselves. At the lunches there are presentations and we have conversations around the room about teaching and learning. Our staff does present to faculty. We have ongoing training. But as a group, every week we hold teaching sessions for ourselves to teach or to play a game demo, and every other week we meet on a program level.

In addition, department managers must be able to act as *advocates*. This might mean dispelling myths or taking the side of the under-represented or under-appreciated party. Any opinion coming from the IDD team that instructor-experts have nothing to contribute to the design side should be quashed. Instructor-experts who don't see the value of the design team should be educated in designers' roles and abilities, and encouraged to open up to opportunities outside the traditional paradigm.

Managers need to be able to tell an IDD team member or instructor-expert, "If that's how the person is behaving, I'll go talk to their boss and figure things out."

The managers of programs with successful ILO initiatives tend to:

1. Brand and market the ILO development program so as to promote transformational teaching and learning.

2. Recruit, assess, hire, and assemble IDD project teams consisting of highly skilled professionals.

3. Convene program-level conferences or meetings.

4. Establish both standards of quality and goals for continuous improvement.

5. Continuously evaluate both individual projects and the program as a whole in light of the program's quality standards and stated values.

6. Encourage the professional development of individual IDD team members specific to their titles and skill sets.

7. Ensure that IDD team members adhere to program-level standardization of processes and tools.

8. Establish benchmarks of success through the expectation of achievement. Make it a goal to create award-winning ILOs, and to generate every product on schedule. Recognize quality, and celebrate success.

9. Make instructor-experts feel that they are critical to the IDD team's process.

10. Model the behavior expected of micro-collaborators.

11. Organize a cadre of faculty members whom the IDD team can consult, and who will serve as ambassadors of online learning.

Overview

No part of developing an ILO happens in isolation. It requires micro-collaboration from beginning to end. In turn, micro-collaboration requires (1) the *personal* efforts of project members and (2) the *organizational* efforts of program/department managers. Designers need to commit to actively enhancing their professional/theoretical acumen; instructor-experts need to recognize that the knowledge of the IDD team is not subordinate, but complementary to their own. Managers at the program/department level need to promote high standards of professionalism and facilitate *mutual* sharing—both between individual designers and between IDD teams and instructor-experts. By following the strategies laid out in this chapter, the various participants in an ILO initiative will acquire many of the *tools* for micro-collaborating while building a *level playing field* on which those tools can have the greatest effect.

<<MICRO-COLLABORATION IN PRACTICE>>
By Jon Aleckson with Kathleen M. Edwards, CAE
Coaching Instructor-Experts, or SMEs

"Successfully working with SMEs comes down to building and sustaining relationships," says Kathi Edwards. "Creating learning is a partnership between SMEs and the IDD team, and you can't have effective partnerships without quality relationships."

In the business world (business being used in the broadest sense, meaning private companies, associations, non-profits, etc.), "subject matter expert" (or "SME") is the widely used term for "instructor-expert." Edwards is a learning consultant who works with business clients to create effective learning environments and strategies; in many cases that means working extensively with SMEs. After 30+ years of facilitating cooperation between SMEs and those who work with them to accomplish learning goals, she's what might be called an "SME specialist." She has developed and led many workshops and conference sessions for (1) those working with SMEs and (2) SMEs who need or want to learn how to be more effective "facilitators of learning." One recent example is Essentials of Coaching SMEs to Facilitate Learning, a webinar she leads five times per year for ASTD (American Society for Training & Development). In sum, she's well-qualified to talk about micro-collaborative communication and building effective relationships between SMEs and IDD teams.

Edwards emphasizes that while every SME is different in terms of personality and professional obligations, they have many of the same concerns and motivations. To establish an effective micro-collaborative working relationship, find out early on what an individual SME's motivations are, and what questions he or she has about the project and his or her role in it. Also, discover how much time the SME can devote to the project; in the business world, most SMEs won't be getting paid extra for their work on an ILO. Their other responsibilities won't be scaled down and their other deadlines won't be pushed back. They'll have numerous demands on their attention and availability, making their time both scarce and valuable. Achieving a micro-collaborative working relationship means, in part, coming up with realistic expectations for the SME's involvement.

"SMEs and IDD people are usually in different departments, making it important to build awareness of the value of effective communication and encourage its use," says Edwards. "Effective communication enables relationship-building and good relationships enable the teamwork required on learning projects. A good relationship with an SME also helps enable his/her willingness to be coached about effective learning." Edwards recommends being very clear up front about what the SME will be expected to do, and what kind of support he or she will receive during the project. "Because an SME often faces conflicting priorities between the project and a 'real job,' consider drafting a simple letter of agreement between the SME and the IDD leader, perhaps including the SME's supervisor. Such an agreement, spelling out how the micro-collaboration will work and what everyone's role will be, helps the SME understand what he or she is getting into and lays the groundwork for good communication."

Edwards notes that besides being pressed for time, many SMEs have little to no experience with adult learning. This can present quite a challenge for the team as a whole. Hence, Edwards promotes learner advocacy: putting the learner at the core of the project. She guides SMEs in providing content that focuses on the needs of the ILO's intended audience. "Because SMEs have that deep knowledge and passion for their content," Edwards says, "they frequently want to put everything they know about the subject into the ILO. It can be challenging for them to remember what it was like to be a content beginner." She works with them to differentiate between content that is "need-to-know" and content that is "nice-to-know." The former is always included; the latter, only if there is time and space. "This process occurs in both face-to-face and online learning opportunities. It's especially challenging when transforming a face-to-face class into a webinar. Content always takes more time to lead online, and we always need to consider reprioritizing the learning objectives and adjusting the content accordingly."

Distinguishing need-to-know from nice-to-know demands an acute understanding of the program's learning objectives and its intended audience, who, in the business world, are typically working adults. They'll want to be engaged and relate what they're learning to what they do on the job. Accordingly, when SMEs are leading learning opportunities, Edwards encourages them to do less lecturing and more facilitating, actively seeking to engage participants in the learning process. She focuses on coaching SMEs in applying generally accepted adult learning principles/practices, which are derived from Malcolm Knowles' theory of adult education known as "andragogy." Simply stated, this means "chunking" the content into smaller segments interspersed with opportunities for discussion, activities that allow learners to experience/practice what they're learning, and reflection that allows them to begin applying new concepts to their own situations. SMEs that are only providing their content knowledge to the project—i.e., not contributing much to the instructional design stage —also need to understand how adults learn. Why? If SMEs know how their content will be used in the learning setting, it is easier for them to focus on what is "need-to-know" to achieve the learning objectives.

To set the proper stage for coaching, Edwards asks SMEs to fill out a simple self-assessment. The results give her an idea of how SMEs view their expertise and experience as facilitators of learning. For example, to what extent do they see learning as a two-way process? How comfortable are they with engaging learners and effectively using adult learning principles and practices? Ultimately, her goal is to ensure that the learner is front and center during the entire development process. "It's easy," she says, "to forget about the learner during the intense process of designing learning opportunities. Keeping learners-and how they learn-at the forefront every step of the way helps to ensure the resulting product is effective for those who matter most. It's not about the SMEs; it's not about the IDD team; it's about the learners and what is best for them. With every client, I am the learner advocate, and I help the client's team gain and use that perspective as well." For Edwards, then, effective collaboration requires knowledge of where people are coming from and what people need. "When you're developing learning opportunities, a culture in which everyone's willing to learn from everyone else goes a long way towards ensuring success." In her work as an SME specialist, Edwards helps clients overcome roadblocks to mutual learning. Along the way, she's ensuring the SME is both hearing others and being heard—and that learners always come first.

CHAPTER 4

Structure: Project Management and the Development Process

What you look for in project management is a mixture of flexibility and discipline: you need a project manager who can make the most of any situation, and who knows how to get team members to do their best work. At the same time, you need someone who will establish the right process and keep to that process—someone who knows how to run the process in a way that increases repeatability and keeps costs down without sacrificing quality. —*Clark Aldrich*

We have mentioned that micro-collaboration doesn't happen in a vacuum: it is subject to external constraints, particularly constraints related to time and money. Part of successful micro-collaboration is coming up with creative ways to keep external constraints from compromising the team's end product—or, in software development terms, the team's deliverable. How, given limited hours and limited dollars, does anyone generate a high-quality ILO?

The key is project management. ILO initiatives (especially higher-education online-repurposing missions) too rarely assign the role of project manager to someone who has no other hats to wear; instead, they rely on a senior member of the IDD team to keep the project on track, even while he or she attends to more specific design and development issues. In the case of superstar developers like Dave Gagnon and Amy Dietz, this can work, but only some of the time, because even superstars are fallible. Depending on them is not a sustainable strategy, partly because there are too few superstars to go around.

A much more reliable and, often, more effective strategy is to use certain principles and procedures that, if followed by a designated project manager, will keep a project on an even keel—superstars or not. In the end, charisma and passion are excellent qualities for a project manager to have, but they are not as important as understanding the mechanics of teams; i.e., the nuts and bolts of getting a project from start to finish on spec, on time, and on budget.

When it comes to mechanics, efficiency is everything. It falls to project mangers to ensure that meetings are covering new ground rather than getting stuck on moot points, that work assignments are getting done on deadline, and that the instructor-expert's time and energy are being put to good use. They must know every detail of the development process, including the roles of those performing tasks within the process.

In this chapter, we'll look at how project managers establish efficient practices, especially in terms of process. We'll also look at how project managers can play a crucial role in infusing an ILO with the tacit knowledge of the instructor-expert. And, of course, we'll look at some stories from the field, especially the story of how the Cool-It team operated—both where it went right and where it went wrong.

The Triple Constraint

At the heart of project management studies is the triple constraint: the dreaded chimera of schedule/time, scope/quality, and costs/resources, each characteristic tearing viciously at the others, thirsting for blood and hell-bent on destruction...

...until, that is, a knowledgeable project manager comes along and tames it, at which point the triple constraint transforms into an orderly triangle, balanced and non-threatening, each part exerting equal pressure upon its well-behaved peers.

The basics of the triple constraint are self-explanatory: one constraint cannot be changed without changing the other two. Simple geometry. Increased scope/quality = increased cost/resources = lengthened schedule/time.

The project manager's job is to assess the details of his team's situation based on the triangle. Does the project need to get done quickly, and produce a high-quality deliverable? Then throw more people at it—which, of course, will increase the cost, unless getting the project done quickly makes up for the heightened labor expense.

Scope/Quality

Figure 9. The triple constraint.

Identify the project's constraints, manipulate the constraints as advantageously as possible, and provide the tools for the team to organize its work within the constraints' parameters. That, broadly speaking, is what a project manager does.

Articulation and Documentation

To put it a little more specifically, the project manager formalizes the design and development process and communicates it to both the IDD team and-of especial importance-the instructor-expert. This process needs to be documented from the beginning. The entire team needs to be aware of it and, thus, accountable for it.

Of course, some finesse is required. The project manager generally formulates a detailed internal schedule that lists specific tasks and deadlines for designers, and formulates a separate, general overview of that

69

schedule for the instructor-expert and upper management. Each schedule addresses the following points:

1. The project's goals and objectives

2. The scope of the deliverables; on the detailed schedule, a task list for each deliverable

3. Timelines (including a weekly standing meeting, usually conducted virtually)

4. Reporting and evaluation requirements

Some IDD teams create a project charter, a one-page summary of the initiative for distribution to all stakeholders. Others eventually create more specific documents that address the instructional guidelines and technical requirements under which the team is working. It all depends on the complexity of the project: the more people involved and the more interactive the deliverable, the more thorough and voluminous will be the articulation documents. This is usually a given in the corporate world, but is just as important in higher education.

What ILOs Cost

There's a direct relationship between a project's budget and the planning documents it requires. Any ILO costing over $20,000 calls for highly specific articulation of schedules and task assignments. When you're investing a lot of money, you have to be unequivocal about what needs to get done, who needs to do it, when the deadlines are, and how much you're going to spend per task.

Rich, sophisticated ILOs can take between 100 and 1,000 hours to produce. They usually hinge on special grant opportunities or an influx of funds due to corporate re-prioritization. 1,000 hours is a scary number, especially if you allow for $100 per hour, which is a reasonable expectation when you're dealing with contracted corporate ILOs. But a high-quality ILO can be created in fewer than 100 hours if you have the right tools in place. One such tool might be a repeatable template that can be used for multiple courses; on the low end, this could be something as simple as a narrated slide show, while on the high end, it could be a conceptual- or process-map generator.

You can combine templates with online support for collaboration. Web-based systems for authoring and content-management, combined with searchable ILO repositories, can in some cases cut development time in half.

Something for upper-level management to keep in mind is the possibility of amortizing development costs based on per-student-experience over subsequent courses/years.

The Triple Constraint and Micro-collaboration

No matter the financial environment, competent project management paves the way for productive micro-collaboration. It does so in multiple dimensions, with one of the most critical dimensions being the IDD team's aura of professionalism. A well-documented, consistently managed development process will communicate to the instructor-expert that the IDD team knows what it's doing. It's been through this before (or if it hasn't, then it at least has a plan for making things work). It's not going to waste time. Something that can help in this regard is holding a preliminary workshop that covers what, exactly, instructional design and development entails, and also introduces the specific IDD people who will be involved with the project. Such a workshop provides an opportunity to affirm the team's commitment to quality, which should set the tone for future work.

When the triple constraint is managed well from day one, the team is likely to have a clear understanding of the mission, including the relative importance of each part of the mission. This leads to greater efficiency, which, in turn, leads to more time spent with the instructor-expert, mining his or her experience for tacit knowledge. In filmmaking terms, good project management means that more dollars and resources are seen on the screen.

Project management done right promotes confidence and comfort. It convinces the instructor-expert that his or her hours are being put to valuable use. And when the instructor-expert feels that way, he or she is likely to be more forthcoming with tacit knowledge. More invested in the deliverable. The deliverable will be far better for it—far richer, far more immersive, far more engaging. That goes for sixteen-week online courses as much as for simulation-level, skills-training ILOs.

The project manager should set aside time for activities that require micro-collaboration. Such activities need to show up on the schedule, and they need to be facilitated, even if informally. A project manager committed to micro-collaboration will:

1. Schedule creative sessions, or brainstorming meetings, that are organized around learning objectives. They should focus on the ideas of both the instructor-expert and the IDD team. These meetings are ignited by discussing examples of what the IDD team and instructor-expert consider best practice for ILOs; the goal is to set a common bar for group achievement. What will we all take pride in? What can we accomplish if we all remain passionately involved?

2. Keep track of standing meetings: make sure that people attend them, that notes are recorded, and that decisions are honored.

3. Manage document-creation, including the project plan, budget reports, prototype concept storyboards, blueprints of complex simulations, user feedback evaluation documents, code documentation, and summative evaluation documents.

4. Set up blueprinting-document reviews and discussions, especially when it comes to laying out the features/scope of complex ILOs.

5. Establish a consensus on which parts of the ILO will require advanced coding, and what skill set will be required of programmers in implementing the design.

6. Be transparent and precise in version articulation, from prototype to alpha, alpha to beta, and beta to final release.

The Agile Development Process

The project manager needs to keep every member of the team on the same page. Everyone needs to know what's expected of him or her, and when. For that to happen, the instructor-expert needs to understand the basics of instructional systems design. When the philosophy underlying the project's schedule is obscure to the instructor-expert, micro-collaboration suffers. So we'll take some time here to discuss current trends in development models.

To maintain and measure forward progress, the project manager requires a scheme, or model, for getting from point A (no deliverable to speak of) to point Z (a polished deliverable that meets learners' needs). The IDD team will already know, of course, that the old, rigid waterfall models are out of the question, including the younger but still outdated ADDIE (Analysis, Design, Development, Implementation, Evaluation).

Such models were de rigueur in the late 20th century, when Berge and other researchers claimed that a strict division of labor and a linear development process were the best way to achieve collaboration (1995). But in the last decade, research has tended show that "optimization and control" methods are less effective than methods that "encourage learning and innovation" in team members (Nerur and Balijepally 2007).

A new paradigm has come to dominate educational software design. This is because rigid development processes are not conducive to micro-collaboration—or, at the very least, are not designed to reap the benefits of micro-collaboration, even if (like ADDIE) they don't entirely discourage it. An egalitarian team, one built on communication, flexibility, and mutual sharing, requires a model that can accommodate quick changes. A model that won't cause the project to grind to a halt or trudge back to the drawing board when end-user problems are discovered. In short, an egalitarian team needs Agile (or something of that ilk).

The Agile model of software development places great emphasis on how knowledge is shared amongst team members. It stresses the importance of structured activities based on feedback and reflection; these enhance communication within the team, and lead to suggestions on how forthcoming versions of the deliverable can be improved.

The "Manifesto for Agile Software Development," widely known as the Agile Manifesto, was developed by seventeen software developers in 2001. Appropriately, it is not some weighty tome given over to polemics or technicalities, but a short list of priorities meant to redefine how software developers approach their projects:

> We are uncovering better ways of developing software by doing it and helping others do it. Through this work we have come to value:
>
> - *Individuals and interactions* over processes and tools
> - *Working software* over comprehensive documentation
> - *Customer collaboration* over contract negotiation
> - *Responding to change* over following a plan
>
> That is, while there is value in the items on the right, we value the items on the left more. (Beck et al. 2001)

Underlying these priorities are twelve principles that, in the decade since their introduction, have become watchwords, if not axioms, for serious game developers (Beck et al. 2001):

1. Customer satisfaction by rapid delivery of useful software

2. Welcome changing requirements, even late in development

3. Working software is delivered frequently (weeks rather than months)

4. Working software is the principal measure of progress

5. Sustainable development, able to maintain a constant pace

6. Close, daily co-operation between business people and developers

7. Face-to-face conversation is the best form of communication [Video conferencing makes face-to-face conversations possible even when the participants are geographically distant.]

8. Projects are built around motivated individuals, who should be trusted

9. Continuous attention to technical excellence and good design

10. Simplicity

11. Self-organizing teams

12. Regular adaptation to changing circumstances

How Agile Works

In more concrete terms, Agile is the process of creating many different *iterations* of a deliverable, with each iteration improving on the last. These iterations are produced in discrete, time-boxed efforts. Each time box typically runs from two to six weeks, and at the end of the time box, the new iteration of the deliverable is subjected to user testing. Thus, users are able identify problems with the deliverable, and the team has the chance to solve those problems with the next iteration. This is the definition of "formative evaluation": using evaluations not as a final grade (that would be "summative evaluation"), but as *feedback* that shapes the ultimate version of the deliverable (more on this in chapter 6).

Ideally, an Agile development process includes a set number of time-boxes; after the last one, you've got a deliverable that meets all, or nearly all, of your users' needs. With an old waterfall or ADDIE development process, there was always the chance that after months or years of work, you'd get to the stage of user testing and find that your deliverable didn't do what your learners needed it to. You'd have sunk huge amounts of time and money into a product that didn't work.

Avoiding that scenario is the main reason for using Agile methods. It's a *pragmatic* process that acknowledges the unlikelihood of a team getting everything right the first time. As Mike Kuniavsky, author of *Observing the User Experience*, puts it:

> Iterative development is based on the idea of continual refinement through trial and error. Rather than trying to create a perfect vision from the beginning, iterative development homes in on the target, refining its focus and perfecting the product until it has reached its goal. Each cycle consists of the same basic steps, and each cycle infuses the product with richer information. (Kuniavsky 2003)

Agile *liberalizes* the process of developing software; it provides an escape route from rigid paradigms in which every step is planned out in exhaustive detail, with little room for change along the way. It connects "knowing and doing (thought and action)," and its value "depends on an organization's ability to nurture learning, teamwork, self-organization, and personal empowerment" (Nerur and Balijepally 2007).

Increasing Interactivity through Agile: Post-iteration Workshops

In order to figure out how to move to the *next* iteration, the team has to talk about the *last* one. Researchers of the Agile development process have found that work habits, learning curves, and the satisfaction of team members all improve when post-iteration workshops are conducted (Salo et al. 2004). These workshops are typically attended by business analysts, instructor-experts, and the development team; sometimes, actual users of the software are invited to weigh in.

As for how such meetings play out, David Talby and fellow software development researchers have made special note of the K-J method. Named after the Japanese ethnologist Jiro Kawakita, the K-J method calls for "each participant [to list] 3–5 issues about the development process on Post-it notes. The notes are then grouped into positive and negative issues, and the negative issues are prioritized. The high priority items are then discussed by the team and turned into action items for changing the team's behavior" (Talby et al. 2006).

75

In the study from which that quote is drawn, Talby and his fellow authors make reference to Donald Schön, a scholar of reflective practices. Schon claims that a person can keep improving his or her professional skills through the practice of continuous critical reflection; this "reflection-on-action" is all about getting stakeholders to participate in analytical activities that result in new ways of thinking (qtd. in Talby et al. 2006). It can also take place during the development phases of ILOs—that is, it can be used "in action" (Schon qtd. in Merriam and Caffarella 1999).

Formal reflection activities are a crucial part of the teaching/learning transaction that takes place between *all* members of the ILO team (again, we'll go into this further in chapter 7). This transaction is the bedrock of the project, and its cultivation falls to the project manager. When reflection activities are formalized, are built into the team's schedule, Agile development methods can lead to "double-loop learning"; that is, *learning to learn* by combining thought and implementation (Argyris 1991). Chris Argyris provides a succinct insight into double-loop learning:

> To give a simple analogy: a thermostat that automatically turns on the heat whenever the temperature in the room drops below 68 degrees is a good example of single-loop learning. A thermostat that could ask "Why am I set at 68 degrees?" and then explore whether or not some other temperature might more economically achieve the goal of heating the room would be engaging in double-loop learning. (1991)

By making post-iteration reflection a standard part of the development process, the project manager will promote double-loop learning. He or she will help each team member learn from the others. There are, of course, many more tools than the K-J method at the project manager's disposal: studies show that using conceptual maps improves the quality of discussion when it comes to structuring and sequencing learning activities (Inglis 2003). Visio flow charts, custom-made spreadsheets/tables, mind-mapping software, and even morphological matrices can have a similar effect (Fargnoli, Ravida, and Troisi 2006; Inglis 2003).

It's up to the project manager to decide which tools will be most useful to his or her team. When undertaken regularly and diligently, the mutual sharing cultivated by post-iteration reflection will come to characterize all stages of the development process—not just the final step of each time box. This, in turn, will lead *directly* to a more immersive, *richer* ILO, because the instructor-expert's tacit knowledge will have the chance to permeate every level of design.

Project Management as a Keystone of Agile

The flexibility of Agile development is what makes it so attractive. But this very quality can turn into a trap, absent strong project management. Every iteration / time box generated throughout the course of the process will have its own unique triple-constraint triangle; these are microcosmic triangles, and the project manager must constantly navigate the tension between them and the *macrocosmic* triangle of the project as a whole. As Kuniavsky puts it,

> Despite its benefits, iterative development isn't perfect. It creates a lot of uncertainty throughout the process, which can be frustrating to a development team that wants to be able to delve deeply into feature development. It requires discipline and dedicated project management because it can be a complex process that requires every iteration to focus on a subset of the product, when other glaring problems may be screaming for attention. (Kuniavsky 2003)

For Agile development to work to its fullest potential, the team needs a dedicated person at the helm, someone who continually relates each iterative time-box to the project's overall schedule. Someone who directs the team's focus to where the need is greatest, depending on the particular iteration on which it's working. If this doesn't happen, then project momentum is likely to suffer. Team members will lose their enthusiasm for contributing ideas—why bother, when they simply get lost in the morass of competing priorities?

Agile development is more subject to entropy; that is, an ever-widening dispersal of energy and attention, of which the above-noted listlessness is but one possible consequence. Without effective project management, the initiative will diminish in efficiency and become a far larger resource drain than intended.

The Engage Program's Iterative Innovation

Agile development can take different forms for different projects. That's what Agile gives you: something dynamic rather than static, malleable rather than ironclad. Agile's capacity to shapeshift presents an early opportunity for project managers to show their mettle: can they tweak the process so that it fits their team? As we mentioned above, tailoring the minutiae of Agile development to the idiosyncrasies of a given team is a crucial part of the project manager's job.

It is fitting, therefore, for us to begin our discussion of Cool-It's development with a brief description of process: Les Howles, staff-anointed arbiter of processes for the Engage program, used a "modified ADDIE." (The Engage program, you'll recall, is the section of UW-Madison's IT Support department that produced Cool-It.) Howles had worked in the private sector before joining Engage; from his experiences there, and from the texts he'd read, he was confident that a departure from the standard ADDIE method would bear fruit. He'd put a lot of thought into the eLearning development process, and knew the importance of collaboration. With that in mind, he provided the Engage team with a one-page handout of his own making (Figure 10).

As you can see, Howles's design process more or less preserves the ADDIE steps. He simply situates them on an iterative trajectory. Based on his knowledge of Engage staff, he felt that this would be enough to foster collaboration while keeping projects on track.

Iterative Design Process for an Instructional Sim-Game

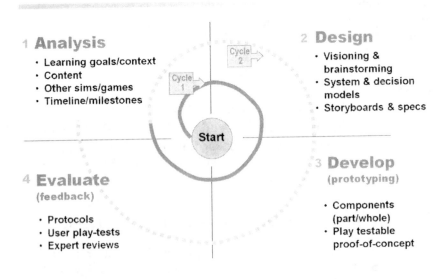

1 Analysis
- Learning goals/context
- Content
- Other sims/games
- Timeline/milestones

2 Design
- Visioning & brainstorming
- System & decision models
- Storyboards & specs

Cycle 2

Cycle 1

Start

4 Evaluate
(feedback)
- Protocols
- User play-tests
- Expert reviews

3 Develop
(prototyping)
- Components (part/whole)
- Play testable proof-of-concept

Figure 10. The modified ADDIE. ©2007-2010 The Board of Regents of the University of Wisconsin System.

"This was new," said Dave Gagnon. "My prior work at DoIT was . . . you hold a brainstorming session and you push that product to the end. What Les wanted us to do was use a repeating ADDIE model. A user-centric design. Instead of starting with subject/content perspective, he laid out a charge for us: 'Start with the user. What do the students see?' [We had to] design from that perspective."

Howles, however, was not the manager of the Cool-It project; he generated process paradigms on the *program* level. This is a good example of creating a *culture* conducive to micro-collaboration (see chapter 3), but when it came to Cool-It, Howles's job did not include overseeing the details of successive iterations. That fell to Gagnon, the project manager / instructional designer.

The Polymath

In face-to-face interviews, the first thing one notices about Dave Gagnon is that he's passionate about his work. It's impossible to miss his ebullient enthusiasm—and little wonder, considering his history. Gagnon's educational background is in computer science. For a time, he owned a video production business. He worked for DoIt in a support capacity, and, during the period of Cool-It's development, was involved with the Games, Learning, and Society MA track within UW-Madison's Curriculum and Instruction program. Hence, Gagnon joined Engage knowing that it would be an arena in which he could exercise many of his skills and explore many of his interests. As he recalls, "It was like, *really?* This is going to be my *job?*"

As we saw in chapter 3, Gagnon's Cool-It colleagues thought highly of him. Both Mike Litzkow (the programmer) and John Pfotenhauer (the instructor-expert) called him "a high-energy person... a person who is a lot of fun and very interesting, with the ability to draw on outside resources to get the job done." Chris Blakesley, the production assistant, considered him "a renaissance man." Indeed, Gagnon has something of the polymath about him. He's gifted with enough right- and left-brain moxie to contribute to a project on both the dynamically creative side (e.g., communicating with artists) and the analytical design side (e.g., communicating with programmers).

Few people have this capacity. It's one of the reasons people respond to Gagnon so well. It's why he's considered a superstar.

Document Storage as a Way of Managing Micro-collaboration

We've been referring to Gagnon as the combined instructional designer / project manager. It's true he had to wear both hats: he was responsible for establishing *features* of the ILO that would accomplish Pfotenhauer's pedagogical goals, and also responsible for keeping the project on spec, on time, and on budget. They weren't unrelated, but they did involve different skills, different strategies. When it came to project management, Gagnon was explicit about the need for micro-collaboration. He wrote in an email,

1. DIVERSE members of a working team

2. are able to SHARE their expertise

3. in such a way that EMERGENT ideas/designs are created and

4. no one member can claim OWNERSHIP.

A crucial step in accomplishing these concatenated goals was keeping detailed notes and posting them on the DoIt Wiki. The Wiki was particularly useful during Phase III of Cool-It's development, when a new version of the ILO came out on an almost weekly basis. Wiki storage served as a repository from which the IDD team could access all project-related communications, articulation documents, and iterations of the deliverable. This helped Gagnon to organize the project's direction and monitor its momentum.

"It kept everyone thinking about the big picture," Gagnon said. "And every week, we asked 'What are we going to do next?' By having access to all information, it made meetings flow very easily; at the very end of the meeting we would put [up] a list of the things we wanted to build and get an idea of how much money it was going to cost and decide how much money we wanted to spend."

Easy, democratic access to information encourages the free flow of ideas. It's one of the reasons Gagnon was so successful at creating an egalitarian project atmosphere, and it led, as we know, to an ILO that was suffused with Pfotenhauer's tacit knowledge of cryogenics. The project was on spec. Unfortunately, it was off in other areas.

The Problem with Dual Roles

Gagnon viewed the role of project manager as something he could handle on a second-nature basis. We've seen that when it came to fostering micro-collaboration, he was right. But project management also requires attention to time and budget—the other two legs of the triple constraint. Cool-It, while a great example of the fruits of micro-collaboration, did not do very well in these other areas. It took around three years to complete, and cost far more than expected.

Our purpose in pointing this out is not to bash Gagnon, who, as we've said, has earned tremendous respect from his colleagues and is uncommonly gifted. Rather, we mean to say that project management can be challenging even for superstars; therefore, it's better for the project as a whole if the manager only has to wear one hat. Gagnon, remember, was both project manager and instructional designer. During year-end evaluations in 2007 and 2008, Engage management themselves wondered whether this duality of roles was a good idea (University of Wisconsin-Madison 2011b). In fact, both IDD team members and instructor-experts claimed to have observed deficiencies in several areas related to project management: budget control, the articulation of requirements, scheduling, and communication with instructor-experts regarding their expectations.

Not all these observations apply to Cool-It: during the years in question, many different projects fell under the Engage umbrella, many different people managed them, and several besides Cool-It ran into problems with the triple constraint. Tellingly, it was common for project managers to wear two hats, with the second one usually related to design and development. We cannot be surprised that problems arose, or that Engage staff wanted more training on how projects should be run (University of Wisconsin-Madison 2011b).

Overall, Engage is a very successful program; it serves as a positive example in most respects. If some of its projects took too long and cost too much, then that should serve to indicate the difficulty of project management, which is so great that even superb individuals and organizations struggle with it from time to time.

Overview

The role of project manager is complex and demanding, so much so that it should be considered a stand-alone job. And precisely because it's so challenging, project management is a locus of opportunity. A dedicated project manager—whose focus is not diffused by other responsibilities—can have a huge impact on the look and feel of the finished ILO. We saw that the egalitarian environment fostered by Dave Gagnon contributed to an engrossing, highly effective product; it should be clear that the decisions of the project manager play a vital role in eliciting the instructor-expert's tacit knowledge. Process-related decisions—e.g., using Agile and tailoring it to fit the needs of the team—are some of the biggest: the project manager's guidance on the process level can make or break a deliverable. By maintaining active communication between team members and coordinating the variables of the triple constraint, the project manager can vastly increase the likelihood of a great ILO coming in on time, on spec, and on budget. In the next chapter, we'll delve deeper into some of the specifics of how to promote communication and continually share expertise.

<<MICRO-COLLABORATION IN PRACTICE>>
By Jon Aleckson with Clark Aldrich
Articulation Documents and the Long-Term Vision

Clark Aldrich sees himself as a "gadfly" of the "Educational Industrial Complex" (2010). Nevertheless, his prolific writing on creating educational games and simulations is widely cited by traditional academics. Aldrich believes strongly in the importance of good project management for:

1. setting team members' expectations throughout development,

2. keeping budgets and planning in perspective,

3. preventing the team from getting lost in the woods and bogged down, and

4. ensuring that the team is doing things in the right order.

To orient a team during the early design stages, Aldrich uses a basic model of Actions, Systems, and Results. If we apply his model to, say, a chemistry course, we'll be asking things like, "What chemicals do we want the students to work with? What actions can they perform with those chemicals that will bring them to an understanding of the concepts? If we want them to create an explosive compound, what kind of reaction, or process, or *system* has to intervene between the action of mixing the chemicals and the outcome (the explosion)? What's the educational value of seeing that process through from start to finish?"

The chemistry example is apt in that Aldrich sees ILOs as being especially well suited to education in science, technology, engineering, and mathematics. ILOs give learners the chance to play around, to experiment with equipment and materials in ways that might be silly or even dangerous in the physical world while being fun and informative in a simulation. The opportunity to mess with the content in a relatively irreverent way makes learners more comfortable with the concepts involved.

Moreover, allowing learners to experiment with the content in an emotional/narrative context can have immediate effects on their real-life decision making (as in the World Anti-Doping Agency's Play True challenge). Project management is crucial here: you don't want the ILO's narrative to be trite, and the first part of getting beyond triteness is developing a concept document (see the online appendix). A concept document generally runs from five to ten pages, and its purpose is to encapsulate the look and feel of the ILO, including the outlines of the narrative. The concept document will often be paired with a 10 to 25-page PowerPoint that provides a more detailed example of a *segment* of the ILO. Given the time and budget, it's a good idea to create multiple concept packages from which the team can choose the best one or two.

Concept documentation is almost always a turning point in the team's momentum. It creates a sense of concrete accomplishment, particularly for the instructor-expert, who can go over each page/slide and make suggestions for improvement. In terms of the instructor-expert's input, the project manager will want to highlight the significance of each part of the concept package: this is important lead-up material, this is a pre-experiment decision point that will affect the later outcome, etc. The concept package is usually the point at which the instructor-expert moves away from the idea of the ILO as a linear representation of best practice, and moves toward thinking of it as a collection of hypothetical scenarios, some of which would be disastrous in real life.

Aldrich writes (2011):

In [the] concept document, include:

1. Introduction
2. Learning Objectives
3. Setup/story
4. Basic gameplay
5. Basic screen interfaces and interactions
6. Basic feedback and reward system

The overview of underlying mechanisms tends to be written more from a *descriptive* than technical perspective. In many ways the combination of the walk-through and the concept document can be viewed as an internal marketing pitch to build common understanding and support."

After the concept package comes the detailed, comprehensive design blueprint. It lays out the functions and levels of the ILO, which helps keep the scope from getting wildly ambitious (an undesirable side effect of the instructor-expert's otherwise desirable enthusiasm). According to Aldrich, the design blueprint should be about 30 pages long and discuss (2011):

1. Overview and rationale

2. Intended audience

3. Learning goals

4. Program goals

5. Core gameplay (including screen shots and storyboards)

6. Level breakouts, sequence, and timing (including story, characters, trailer/entice mode)

7. Evaluation and metrics strategy

8. Distribution / technology environment / SCORM and LMS integration

9. 508 considerations

10. Milestones / project management (including what has been done so far)

11. Bibliography

12. Appendix: high-level overview and examples of mechanisms, including state charts and equations

13. Appendix: analysis of target content

From here, the team moves on to building prototypes.

The project manager's position throughout the development process is dichotomous: he or she needs to be directed and directive at the same time. The team has to have order, has to have a set way of doing things, but the project manager also has to come across as someone who's there to help, or facilitate, rather than boss people around. The project manager maintains the infrastructure without holding too much sway over creative decisions. It's a balancing act.

Academic culture places a high value on perfectionism, and as a result, instructor-experts in academia have a tendency to equivocate when it comes to critical decisions. Their interest is in getting every detail exactly right. That's not bad in and of itself, obviously, but if it leads to the deferment of development commitments, then much of the process will end up getting crammed into the last few weeks before the beginning of the semester. The ILO will suffer. There are many junctures along the road to completion at which the instructor-expert has to commit a certain option: the characters, the scenarios, etc. The project manager's job is to ensure that those decisions are being made in a timely way, such that each stage of the process is respected. This speaks to the professionalism of the IDD team; a clear process at the outset doesn't mean much if it falls into shambles a month down the road.

Therefore, the project manager's main concern is with providing the tools and the overarching guidance necessary to keep the ILO moving at a certain pace toward a certain goal without getting sidetracked or mired. The right attitude toward authority and the right documents make it much easier for project managers to be successful.

CHAPTER 5

Culture:
Creating a Shared Language
for Micro-collaborative
Communication

I find that having things like visual aids, even sketches
on paper or on the whiteboard, can help move a meeting
forward. And what's best is if you start the project by
talking about and looking at programs that exist already.
You want things you can refer back to, especially
mechanics you can identify and say, "That's what we
want ours to do." —*David Gagnon*

When asked how to successfully micro-collaborate, people who have
worked on ILO projects tend to emphasize mutual sharing and good communication. These are fairly obvious factors: how could *any* type of collaboration occur in their absence? For a micro-collaborative enterprise, mutual
sharing and good communication are absolute necessities. That's a given.

However, obviousness doesn't always indicate *ease*. As noted in the
preceding chapters, team members' ability to share their expertise with
one another depends on certain conditions. Some of those conditions are
program-level, and rest on the decisions of upper management (e.g., how
the IT program is branded and marketed). Some are project-level, and rest
on the decisions of the project manager (e.g., how the design and development process is implemented). Mutual sharing and good communication
don't always come naturally: more often, they require conscious, concerted effort from all stakeholders in an ILO project.

The payoff of such concerted effort is a smooth transfer of the instructor-expert's knowledge from the lecture hall or conference room to
the deliverable. This not only *requires* good communication, but also *nour-
ishes* ongoing communication. It creates enthusiasm; it stokes momentum.

We've already looked at some of the ways in which managers (at both the program and department level) can create favorable conditions for micro-collaboration. In this chapter, we'll go into some of the most critical problems that good communication solves. We'll look at examples of how such communication works in real-life, concrete situations. We'll also provide some strategies for team members that, when employed, will pave the way for good communication throughout the development process.

The Artifacts
of Healthy Meetings

The first step of successful communication (and a prerequisite for the effective use of communication tools) is making sure that all team members show mutual respect, offer only constructive criticism, and withhold judgment—especially during brainstorming (see the online appendix for detailed brainstorming rules). It's important to say right up front that everyone's opinion is valuable, that everyone brings a useful perspective to the table and has the freedom to participate without being penalized. Since meetings often favor people who are comfortable speaking in front of groups, it can helpful to use something like the K-J method, which allows team members to write their contributions down. This environment promotes trust and thus enhances the instructor-expert's contribution, as we'll discuss below.

Having established the right ground rules, the team needs to deploy the right artifacts, or tools. These are of particular importance when it comes to official meetings of the project team; in fact, regularly scheduled meetings are themselves a crucial element of good communication. A well-run meeting will usually follow a precise agenda (with the minutes recorded for later reference). It will not consist of team members sitting around a table and sporadically firing off suggestions or voicing complaints. Rather, it will make use of tools that promote *structured interactivity*: documents outlining the requirements of the version or feature under discussion; storyboards; visual representation software (mind mapping, workflow diagrams, morphological matrixes); or even simple brainstorming/whiteboarding techniques.

Using such tools makes communication more focused, more efficient. Workflow diagrams, for instance, lay out tasks to complete in relation to a specific feature of the ILO. They might illustrate the ILO's graphic user

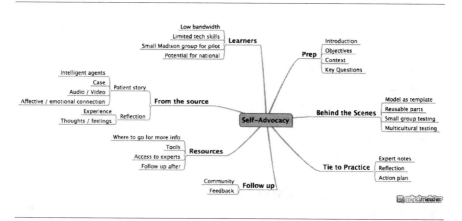

Figure 11. An example of a mind map derived from a brainstorming session.

interface, or the forking decision-paths a learner can take to reach a feature's culmination.

The point of using communication artifacts during meetings is to keep everyone on the same page. The team should be encouraged to raise questions, concerns, or insights that are germane to the meeting's topic while holding off on questions, concerns, or insights that are tangential or completely irrelevant. If the bulk of a meeting is devoted to rehashing old points or deciding whose issues are most important, then people will get frustrated. Especially the instructor-expert, who will have many commitments unrelated to the ILO and—in most cases—won't want to waste a single minute retracing previous discussions. Keeping meetings on track indicates the professionalism of the IDD team and will help get the instructor-expert excited about the project. That, as we know, is a big step toward generating a sophisticated ILO.

Streamlining the discussion topics during meetings is not about denigrating or sidelining people's voices. On the contrary, it's about recognition: the recognition that effective communication requires knowing *what* to talk about, and *when*. In order to know those things, team members must have a crystal-clear understanding of a meeting's purpose and an equally clear understanding of how they're expected to contribute to that purpose. Tightly run meetings that make use of the right communication artifacts lead to stronger collaboration.

Using Visual Aids to Communicate More Effectively

People usually learn better from a combination of text and images than from text alone. The cliché is apt: a picture is worth a thousand words. But how often do team members emerge from meetings with diagrams, or even notes? How often do they return to their desks with flip charts to record their progress, or jpegs of the whiteboard? Based on personal experience . . . not enough.

Visual aids, especially those that can be revisited after the meeting is adjourned, can condense complicated ideas, making them more digestible and more memorable. It may not always seem that way: one IT staff member, when asked about visual aids, claimed, "no one can easily 'read' my drawings," or complex flow charts, "and no one uses them." But when prompted to reflect on whether his visual aids had clarified misunderstandings, or provided a starting point for brainstorming, this same staff member realized that what he'd thought of as useless diagrams had actually made it easier for the team to discuss the details of the project.

The best visual aids get their points across clearly and immediately. However, it's difficult for someone who's not a gifted artist to convey complex ideas with a single, elegant image. Members of an ILO team shouldn't set the bar that high. Things like flow charts and mind maps, though they may appear tangled at first glance, are sufficient to allow each group member to:

1. acquire a sense of the big picture, and

2. zoom in on details to get clarification, establish context, and reach a consensus.

Based, again, on personal experience, the meeting agenda is an excellent site at which to merge visualization with note-taking. Creating the agenda on an electronic platform allows you set off every item with a unique image and add notes to the image as the meeting progresses. This seems to keep people focused. Moreover, if the team knows that the meeting will include some sort of collaborative visual aid (a slide show, for instance), then each member may be motivated to contribute a picture, a sketch, or a chart to represent his or her perspective.

The formats may vary from team to team and project to project, but visual aids always help drum up enthusiasm, keep people focused, and preserve decisions.

Overcoming Didacticism
by Discussing Learning Theories

Flattening power relationships, or creating an egalitarian team atmosphere, renders communication more micro-collaborative than hierarchical. Team members lean toward making suggestions and exchanging
feedback, and lean away from relaying orders or handing down fiats. As we
discussed in chapter 3, a major step toward flattening power relationships
is getting the instructor-expert to see the teaching/learning transaction in
a non-traditional light. The IDD team needs to use its expertise to *per-
suade* the instructor-expert that an ILO is more than just an electronic lecture with fun graphics—that an ILO is, instead, a species of pedagogy in
which the means *become* the end. (This is more true of some ILOs than
others—as we saw, ILOs can be situated on a graph of complexity. In prin-
ciple, however, the centrality of interaction is applicable to *all* ILOs.)

Instructor-experts come to the table with huge amounts of *data*.
They wouldn't be part of the team if it weren't for their intimate familiar-
ity with the subject matter. They have, in other words, a wealth of *explicit*
knowledge, a broad base of information—and in some cases, they want the
ILO to *say* what they know. They want features that will *tell* the learner
what's in the instructor-expert's head, text-heavy items like histories of
the classical musicians, lengthy scripts to be delivered by in-game tutors,
or exhaustive glossaries of technical vocabulary.

Not every instructor-expert feels that way, obviously, but it's a common perspective. When faced with it, it's easy for the IDD team to think
of instructor-experts' attachment to standard lecture materials as
obstinacy or a lack of imagination. That's an unfortunate error. In fact, instructor-experts' apparent attachment to lecture materials may stem from unclear communication of the project's goals—that is, unclear communication of what a good ILO looks like, which is the IDD team's bailiwick.

If an instructor-expert is focused on standard lecture material, it is
the IDD team's responsibility to communicate that *didactic overloads*,
while information-rich, are actually detrimental to the instructor-expert's
learning objectives. A large quantity of information will not be an effective
teaching tool if presented as a block of text or protracted video sequence.
The method by which learners encounter information determines how
much of that information they will assimilate and retain; didactic methods
might work well enough in lecture halls or conference rooms, but when it
comes to eLearning, they eat up resources without yielding results.

The strongest argument for using less didactic, more interactive (or, to use a venerable term, dialectical) teaching methods goes back to our discussion of video game mechanics in chapter 2. A good ILO departs drastically from, say, a lecture-based syllabus or a training slide show. In such didactic settings, the learner's role is one of *passive absorption*; he or she is, ideally, a sponge. By contrast, an ILO based on dialectical pedagogy demands *active absorption*; the ideal learner is inquisitive and eager to experiment.

As we saw in chapter 2, one way of framing the difference between didactic and dialectical pedagogy is to refer to theory—specifically, to the theoretical intersection of video game mechanics and adult learning principles (i.e., constructivist and situational). Kurt Squire, James Gee, and Clark Aldrich are just a few of the many theorists who have addressed how the structure of video games promotes adult learning principles: self-direction, active inquiry, motivation, and individuality in learning tasks (cf. Merriam and Caffarella 1999). Through video game mechanics, ILOs embody adult learning principles by making learning synchronous with doing.

The IDD team must have the theoretical acumen necessary to situate ILOs in a conversation about active learning. This book is not, of course, intended as a primer on education or game theory, but as a practical guide to micro-collaboration, one that draws from and points to theoretical studies. Therefore, let us emphasize that *knowing* theory isn't enough. It's a great idea to highlight passages of Clark Aldrich and show them to the rest of the team, but that alone doesn't constitute micro-collaborative communication. Discussing theory is not an end in itself, but a means of getting the entire team on the same page, a means of homing in on a single, collective expectation of what the final deliverable will offer.

Theory is useful for setting the terms of team discussions and, equally, for inspiring team members to think creatively about pedagogy. The question of pedagogy and its implications for the ILO should be a routine topic, a junction point at which IDD team members and the instructor-expert can swap ideas. No one should tip-toe around it; everyone should feel able to weigh in. This will help the team establish a shared language[1] for talking about the ILO, and may lead to innovations in design.

---

[1] "Each [micro-collaborator] makes use of a specific technical language, so that misunderstanding can easily endanger successful development. In fact, we cannot give for granted that a Literature professor with an educational background understands the [terms] 'active learning' or 'creative discussion' in the same way as a Web programmer does . . . [Yet] the quality of the educational experience heavily depends on the communication between the two . . . These problems clearly call for the definition of a *lingua franca* among the different profiles involved in instructional design" (Botturi 2006).

The Cool-It team, for instance, spent a fair amount of time considering the differences between how novices and experts learn. This resonated with the work of Richard Halverson, associate professor at UW-Madison and co-author (with Allan Collins) of *Rethinking Education in the Age of Technology: The Digital Revolution and Schooling in America* (2009). In the end, it led the team to design a feature that captures learners' decision-making processes and compares them to an expert's. As we noted earlier, this feature makes it possible to establish quantitative maps of learners' progress from neophytism to proficiency.

Enthusiasm, Storytelling, and Tacit Knowledge

Developing a shared language streamlines communication. It creates comfort; it breeds rapport. A sense of rapport completely transforms the way team members talk to one another. Their sentences go from ponderous, planned, and highly technical to quick, fluid, and spontaneous. When two voices overlap, they're as likely to be in harmony as in competition. Taking the time to work out collective expectations and reference points has concrete, observable effects on meeting dynamics.

When team members feel comfortable and enthusiastic in conversation, they develop a sense of personal investment in the project. A particularly auspicious sign of personal investment is *storytelling*. If team members can relate their own experiences to the ILO project, it will create a sense of community, a sense that goes hand in hand with micro-collaboration.

Storytelling is, furthermore, one of the best possible vehicles for communicating expertise. Especially when it comes to tacit knowledge. As Roger Schank puts it, "Communication consists of selecting the stories that we know and telling them to others at the right time. Learning from one's own experiences depends upon being able to communicate our experiences as stories to others" (1990). In a similar vein, Fitzpatrick observes that expert knowledge, being "embodied," must be "trigger[ed] through conversation, through the telling of stories and because of seeing or hearing a connected theme" (qtd. in Ackerman, Pipek, and Wulf 2003).

Tacit knowledge is embedded in real-life experience; it is often entwined with instructor-experts' physical occupancy of specialized spaces, like labs or cockpits; it is always enfolded in instructor-experts' personalities, in how they perceive their environments and how they perceive themselves. That's why tacit knowledge is so hard to convey didactically:

it involves particular people inhabiting particular circumstances. In order to recreate those circumstances virtually—or, depending on resources, to create a more or less faithful facsimile of those circumstances—it's necessary to contextualize them through *narrative*.

We've already discussed the importance of narrative as a design mechanic: if video games teach us anything, it's that people care more about what they're doing when their actions advance a story. When their choices have consequences, good or bad. To create narratives that are both convincing *and* meet the ILO's educational objectives, instructor-experts need to tell their own stories. They need to talk not only about what they do, but about what it's *like* to do it. Says Halverson, "Narratives that capture the critical aspects of context can aim to immerse us vicariously in the habitus of the expert practitioner in order to give access to the practitioner's problem-setting and problem-solving practice" (2004).

Clark Aldrich proposes fifteen questions that will help establish the *specific details* of the instructor-expert's tacit knowledge, the details that set him or her apart from a beginner (2011):

1. Can you think of an experience that epitomized the subject matter? (This could be a real-time meeting or an event that unfolded over weeks, months, even years.)

2. In that situation, what options did you consider to be available to you? Can you go step by step through the actions you took? Would a "naïve" or inexperienced person have acted differently?

3. What things might the naïve approach fail to account for?

4. What are some clues that informed your knowledge of the situation? What did you see immediately, and what did you have to look for? How did you go about looking?

5. What would you have considered to be a successful outcome? Was that the actual outcome?

6. What were you looking for to check whether things were going well? What were you looking for to check whether things were going wrong?

7. What were the "maintenance" or routine activities you had to perform (even down to body language)? What would have happened if you hadn't performed them?

8. When did you know you'd been successful (or hadn't)?

9. If the experience involved other people, what was each person's best-case and worst-case outcome? What were their strategies? What did they do?

10. What are three to five other ways someone could approach the situation and still have a reasonable chance of being successful?

11. What are three to five of the highest-level metrics you were monitoring? Time? Commitment? Alignment?

12. What tradeoffs were you willing to make?

13. Can you graph the high-level metrics over the course of the experience?

14. What were the inflection points for each metric?

15. How did your actions impact the high-level metrics? What else impacted them? (Be as specific as possible.)

Personal Investment, Expertise, and Visualization in Cool-It's Development

To spark micro-collaborative communication, it's helpful to have *exemplars*: games, simulations, or other eLearning activities at which the team can look for inspiration and/or a reality check. Exemplars will prompt the team to talk about things as abstract as genres and as particular as which keys should correspond to what commands. They'll help the team establish the broad conventions and design mechanics with which they're working.

In this respect, the Cool-It team had an auspicious start. Dave Gagnon and John Pfotenhauer came up with an exemplar within ten minutes of meeting each other. "John arrived with an inspiration," recalled Gagnon, "the game *The Incredible Machine*, which is a game I happen to be very fond of ... It's something his kids and he have played. An old, DOS-based game. I had used it in presentations, it's a really good example of a combination sim/game. John said, 'I was inspired by this ... maybe we should consider this.'"

The enthusiasm sparked by this coincidence was reinforced when Gagnon presented Pfotenhauer with a specific design process and started asking him questions related to both content domain and pedagogy; in

95

other words, when he turned conjecture into series of actionable steps. Gagnon was focused, from the beginning, on establishing the project's learning objectives and mapping out the design features by which those objectives could be achieved. He communicated the parameters of the project and worked with Pfotenhauer to create a *common vision* of the final deliverable.

(Initially, Pfotenhauer imagined that Cool-It would contain links to an exhaustive bank of didactic information on cryogenic engineering. Gagnon agreed to put in a placeholder for this bank. Gradually, as the team members hashed out the mechanics of the ILO, it became clear that adding Pfotenhauer's didactic reservoir would double the work of the project. Instead, the team developed the game's "consultant" function, a compromise between the instructor-expert's initial vision and the reality of how games and simulations operate.)

For about three weeks, Gagnon and programmer Mike Litzkow became students of cryogenics: Pfotenhauer explained thermo-contraction, the coefficient of heat transfer, and various material properties, among other things. There were lots of math problems drawn on the board. Gagnon, not admitting the exact extent to which he could follow along,

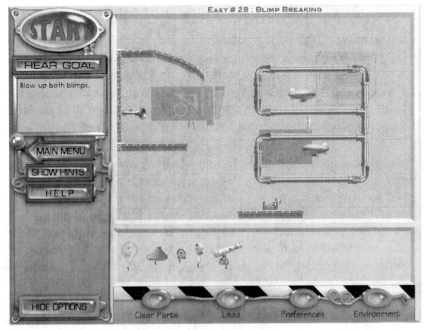

Figure 12. A shot from The Incredible Machine.

said he knew what a differential equation was and figured Litzkow knew how to solve one. This was a big deal, because it was up to Litzkow, the programmer, to code the proper mathematical algorithms into the ILO's software. He had to get them right. If he didn't, the virtual interface gauges would all have the wrong readings; students might make the right choices and get disastrous results, or vice versa, because the mathematical operations underlying the ILO would be off.

"There is a lot to mechanical engineering," said Litzkow, "because you have to build a structure strong enough, but yet because you are trying to minimize heat transfer, you have to make everything long and thin ... Basically, through question and answer, the professor taught me enough about thermodynamics to put a simulation together and model the real world correctly."

The team used a whiteboard to explore the mathematical principles of cryogenics engineering. They photographed their equations and drawings and uploaded them to the project site's Wiki for later reference. "What I did," said Pfotenhauer, "is I brought in a list of the type of problems that I would envision incorporating into the game. We just talked through them. And [Gagnon] did a lot of drawing on the whiteboard and I did to, and we just interacted to describe the scenarios, various stories on the board. And we also, on the whiteboard, played around a lot, a lot of brainstorming, as far as the format, the layout of the game, what kind of features it would have, how one thing would feed into another."

The team members agreed that writing or drawing out their ideas on the whiteboard improved the flow of their communication. It encouraged suggestions and inspired spontaneous creativity. "I think it is really important to get visual," said Gagnon, "and when you have sketches on a whiteboard, everyone has to interact with it, and we know if we are on the same page or not, because we can see it." They established *common reference points*[2].

"During those brainstorming sessions," recalled Pfotenhauer, "you had everything going on at the same time. You had the gaming-like features; we'd toss those around amongst us. I would instruct them about the content, technical content, and they caught on to that pretty quick. And

---

[2] "What is not needed is a canned set of symbols, like logos, icons, templates, or emoticons, but a broad based development of representational or generational skills: skills at conceptualizing, summarizing, editing, communicating, organizing, ordering, and structuring for instructional designers. In simpler terms, instructional designers need to draw to plan, to conceive, and to communicate" (Hokanson 2007).

then, what was really fun was, as Mike would start doing the programming, he would come back, telling me how things were behaving. And he was, at that point, learning the technical subject matter, and it was really fun to see him tell Dave and the other guys in the room, 'No, no, it works like this,' because he had interacted with it. And it was at that point that I could say, 'Yeah, this game is working.'"

Whiteboarding was only part of the team's micro-collaborative communication; you may recall from chapter 2 that Gagnon and Litzkow visited Pfotenhauer in the lab to watch him work. Pfotenhauer was committed to sharing not only his explicit knowledge, but also his worldview and professional environment. This contributed directly to the construction of Cool-It's narrative, especially the realism of its cut-scenes. Pfotenhauer suggested that when designing cut-scenes, the IDD team work with some of his laboratory students who had experience with 3D modeling programs. These students were in an excellent position to combine Pfotenhauer's *expert* experience of the lab with the IDD team's *novice* experience of it. Once they had generated 3D models, Gagnon hired freelance artists who could translate them into video form.

Thus, the formulation of Cool-It's narrative elements involved the team members sharing their interests, situating their knowledge in real-life environments, and using their personal connections to bring whiteboard brainstorming sessions to fruition.

Technological and Process-based Support for Communication

We can't say with certainty how any particular team will get along. People are complex, and have wildly different ways of interacting. Certain tools, however, can increase teams' ability to micro-collaborate. There will be teams out there that are so dysfunctional as to be beyond help, no matter the tools; there will also be teams that are so effortlessly productive that they can do good work even with few tools at their disposal. But such teams are at the extreme ends of the bell curve. For the many others in between, using the following tools can help turn mediocre micro-collaboration into excellent micro-collaboration. Note that they overlap considerably with our tools for effective project management; this should indicate the strong interrelationship between the five factors that make micro-collaboration possible.

Project schedule, process, and approval-point document. The purpose of this document is to lay out, in written form, the stages of development, iterative processes, user-testing dates, and reviews/approvals needed of the instructor-expert.

Document preservation. Establish a repository website or server file structure on which to store documents and photos related to various stages of the project. This might be a Wiki, a blog, a unique domain name, or a Content Management System course container.

Audience profiling. Research the target audience to determine effective writing styles and design approaches.

Benchmarking and brainstorming. Conduct creative sessions where high-quality, similarly budgeted ILOs or online courses are examined. Use this stage for discussions of interactivity standards, and theories that relate to active learning.

Concept approval. Record stakeholders' approval of final concepts using a standard form, one that outlines the look and feel, features, functionality, and visual elements of the ILO.

Blueprints. For elaborate ILOs like games and simulations, blueprints run to around thirty pages.

Scripting/copywriting. Draft the content for all of the ILO's features; e.g., syllabi, job aids, tutorial scripts, audio scripts, video scripts, and instructor resources. This will provide opportunities to talk about didactic vs. dialectical pedagogy.

Technical specifications document. Might be required if you anticipate server-side programming and web browser usage.

Software and art. Use scratch graphics and rough copy in early iterations to indicate how the ILO's content will be expressed through programming; this will illuminate certain pedagogical questions, among other things.

Project team site. Use a website to conduct day-to-day stakeholder communications. The functionality of this site should allow for (1) version control of documents using a dedicated management system; (2) discussion forums to ensure transparency, accountability, and access to all members of the team, reducing reliance on email for important exchanges; and (3) project goals that are set on a weekly basis and automatically emailed to all team members.

Weekly progress meetings and web-based conferencing. Make decisions collectively, review the week's work, and set expectations and goals for the coming week. Have a "business" portion of the meeting and a creative portion. Share a visual agenda, project progress, and relevant images. Take

Figure 13. An online project team site that uses open-source LMS software. Project files are housed in what otherwise would be called a "course." Push email technology allows stakeholders to receive weekly email updates.

notes together and post them to the team site for access and review. Confirm in writing those items that require action before the next meeting.

Project management software. Use formal scheduling software for both internal and external turnarounds. It should allow for automatic schedule adjustments when deadlines are altered.

Authoring software. Web-based authoring software is becoming more and more common. It has the potential to improve micro-collaboration by allowing team members to access the ILO from anywhere at any time.

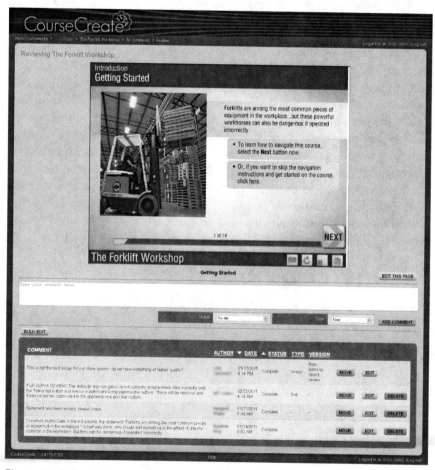

Figure 14. ILO development is moving from working on an individual desktop to web-based authoring that allows all team members to work simultaneously. This system lets instructor-experts comment on a page in context, as the ILO is being developed. System © 2011 Web Courseworks, Ltd. ILO © 2011 JJ Keller & Associates.

This increases the project's overall efficiency, allows for clearer in-context communication, and makes best use of the instructor-expert's time (which will make him or her much happier in the long run).

Overview

It's practically impossible to create a high-quality ILO in the absence of good communication between team members. Broadly speaking, good communication consists in two elements: refined focus on the project's objectives, and the free flow of ideas and stories. There is a certain tension between these elements. If the former (the focus on objectives) is too stringent, team members may end up second-guessing their contributions to meetings, which will stifle creativity. If the latter (the free flow of ideas and stories) is too permissive, meetings may be derailed by endless personal anecdotes, which will diminish productivity. Strike the right balance, and the tension between the two elements of good communication will become *galvanizing*. It will lend shape and impetus to meetings, stimulating innovation and spurring momentum. Using the tools and strategies discussed above will make the difference between lackluster conversations and the type of dynamic, micro-collaborative communication that leads to high-end deliverables. In the next chapter, we'll examine how micro-collaborative communication can be made to have the strongest possible effect on iterative design.

<<MICRO-COLLABORATION IN PRACTICE>>
By Jon Aleckson with Les Howles and Brad Hughes
Conversation Engines, Decision Points, and Design Templates

When UW's Writing Center wanted to build a training tool for its grad-student tutors, it turned to the Engage program. Les Howles (who designed the program's "modified ADDIE" development process, as noted in chapter 4) was put in charge of the project. The goal was to create a computer simulation capable of providing an immersive, situated practice environment that would teach tutors how to talk to students who needed help with their writing. Eventually, this project yielded what Engage calls the "Case ScenarioBuilder," or CSB. The story of the CSB team aptly demonstrates the way in which game-design theory, through visualization and the use of concrete examples, can be combined with learning theory to set the stage for good, micro-collaborative communication.

Brad Hughes, director of the Writing Center and instructor-expert for CSB, knew that effective tutors have the tacit knowledge to help different students in different ways. That is, effective tutors know, based on experience, what type of feedback will be most useful to a given student, and can adjust their behavior accordingly. These adjustments require the tutor to react instinctively to the student's demeanor (including body language), as well as to the particular aims of the student's writing. In Hughes's words:

> One half-hour, [the tutor] is sitting down with a senior who's writing a personal statement for a law school application, and the next half hour they're meeting with a first-year undergrad who's writing their first college paper in a history course . . . In the next hour, they might be meeting with a doctoral student doing a dissertation in civil and environmental engineering about a new way to test the strength of bridges . . . there's just enormous range and variation and so on. And everybody who comes into that consultation, every student writer, has different expectations.

For Les Howles, this meant that the ILO would need to be based on *situational* learning, a challenge for which he was well suited. "Barely a week would go by without [Les] sharing another good article from the educational literature about the power of situational learning," said Hughes. "He has a real passion for it."

Hughes, thanks to the collaborative nature of work in the Writing Center, fully expected that micro-collaborative communication would be an essential part of creating a situational ILO. According to him, working on a team entails that "each person brings and contributes specialized knowledge valuable for the project, cares deeply about the quality and success of the overall project, and contributes actively to conversations which generate new ideas and plans. The result of such collaborations is much better than what any one individual could create." It's obvious that when it came to flattening power relationships, Hughes was completely on board: he *anticipated* the IDD team's professional status, and saw their specialized knowledge not as a threat, but as an *asset*.

Howles knew that the development process had to start with brainstorming and benchmarking sessions. The IDD team had to meet with Hughes to determine, collectively, what scenarios to program into the ILO, and to look at examples of high-quality ILOs with similar themes— "sharing exemplars," in Howles's words. Doing so allowed the team to establish multiple options for the ILO's design, and helped them stay true to one of Howles's mantras: "Don't run with the first idea."

To facilitate communication during these meetings, Hughes screened videos of "model" Writing Center consultations, pointing out to the IDD team some subtle behaviors of effective tutors. The IDD team, for their part, presented relevant pieces of ILOs that Engage had created for other departments. In particular, they focused on a tool that DoIT had developed for UW Hospitals' pediatric care—an object with limited branching that contained text, audio, and video to impart soft skills. As a whole, the project team established shared expectations of the ILO using visible examples and real-world stories.

At a later stage in the development process, the IDD team looked to Hughes and his colleague Melissa Tedrowe (associate director of the Writing Center) to come up with realistic dialogue for the ILO's scenarios. They did so—in abundance. "It would go on for pages," says Howles. "What do you do as a designer? You show them examples of how it does not work with scrolling text, and show exemplars, and explain things like: notice when you look at this good design, the response length is equal between parties…If I ran into a good example on the web, I'd do a screen

capture and send it on to them. It is my responsibility to educate faculty. I
know they are too busy to read chapters [of theory], so I'll send segments
[to complement examples from the web]. For example, Clark Aldrich had
a chapter on dialogue in one of his books, and I gave them highlighted sec-
tions of it." The IDD team also brought in a commercial game designer,
who presented examples of simulations that centered on dialogue and
branching, both of which were affected by the learner's choices.

Eventually, Hughes was convinced that long swaths of dialogue
would be detrimental to the ILO. "They'd share articles with us about the
design of simulations," says Hughes. "Lots of them. They would also show
us examples indicating that you can actually put a learner in a situation far
faster than I would have ever thought. So my natural tendency [was] to
think, 'Oh, well, if you [have] a bunch of exposition to do—for example, to
get to a decision point—you have to have all these conversational turns
represented in the simulation. [Now] I don't think you need to have many
of those at all, and I don't think learners want to click through much of
that at all."

The Author Function

Hughes did not want the Writing Center's ILO to be static, but to evolve
continually to reflect tutors' experiences. He wanted his tutors to be able
to write their own dialogue and plan their own scripts following the ILO's
initial release. In addition to making the ILO more comprehensive, this
would give graduate students the chance to learn by teaching—a method
tried and true.

> I do not think that my colleagues and I would ever create the
> platonic ideal of simulations for the kind of learning that goes
> on. I know that personally, my teaching is always changing, so
> I wouldn't want a set of simulations that were fixed and
> couldn't change with me . . . I also deeply, deeply be-
> lieve—and this was in our initial proposal—that once people
> who are using these training materials are experienced, some
> of the best possible advanced training for them would be to
> ask them to create new simulations."

What this required was the creation of an author function, a template
that could be built into the ILO and would allow tutors to write their own
chapters of the simulation. Once built, this template was made available

to professors throughout the campus community. It was applicable to not only the Writing Center, but to just about any course that could make use of the *case method*: presenting students with a problem that might come up in the real world, and asking them to solve it by selecting the correct series of actions. Hence the name "Case ScenarioBuilder."

CSB doesn't *only* facilitate the case method. It can also work as a critical reading tool, allowing professors create e-texts that enhance textbook material with outside links, embedded videos, commentary, etc. But the case method is most interesting to us because it prompts users of CSB to create *branching scenarios*. Simply put, branching scenarios are scenarios that head in different directions based on user input. The user progresses from decision point to decision point by choosing the best of, say, four options. Instructor-experts can, without too much trouble, change the options at any given decision point to fit teaching needs. For a nursing student, a decision point might look like Figure 15.

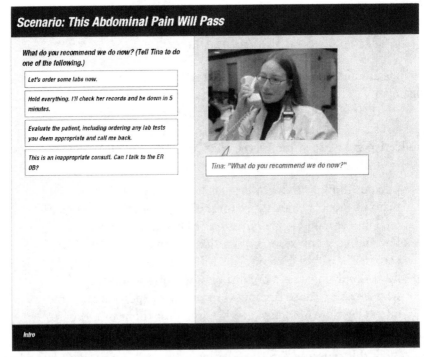

Figure 15. A decision point in an ILO developed for a nursing class using CSB; CSB also includes "after-action support": an authoritative character who provides feedback on the learner's choices.

Whereas a decision point from a different dialogue generator might look like Figure 16.

Developing an author function for the Writing Center constituted a risky spike in the project's scope. But once it was finished and available in its generic CSB form, the author function enhanced communication with instructor-experts on other projects. IDD team members could offer the CSB as a possible way to add interactivity to a course, and could also present the Writing Center's *application* of the CSB as an example of its usefulness. The CSB served to make Engage's work less unfamiliar to instructor-experts; it made communication easier by providing a common starting point for aligning technological tools with learning objectives.

Figure 16. From the World Anit-Doping Agency's PlayTrue Challenge (© 2010); pictured here are some decisions available to players. Conversations branch depending on players' choices. Sports performance statistics appear on the stats card (lower left). Time elapsed during sports events is tracked in terms of money for work events.

CHAPTER 6

Performance: Formative Evaluation

When experts and online media developers decide they
know what's best for learners without taking time, at
each stage of the development process, to actually ask
learners and teachers what works and what doesn't, the
project is doomed to failure or, at best, mediocrity.
—*Dr. Richard Schafer, manager of CHEC BlueKids eLearning
Development*

Micro-collaboration is enhanced when all members of a project team are
encouraged to make suggestions, voice new ideas, and listen to feedback.
Feedback from teachers and students—i.e., the people for whom the ILO
is ultimately intended—is of especial importance. It will be most effective
when the team has a plan for systematically critiquing the deliverable and
implementing new ideas as they emerge. Creating such a plan is, simply
put, the purpose of *formative evaluation*, a term we've used before but
haven't explored in detail.

Formative evaluation is the binary opposite of summative (or post-
mortem) evaluation. The latter occurs only after a deliverable is complete,
and is predominantly retrospective. It answers, "What did we do well, and
what could we have done better?"

By contrast, formative evaluation occurs prior to the deliverable's
completion, and is predominantly prospective. It answers, "What are we
doing well, and what can we do better?"

The difference can be expressed via cooking analogy (Fitzpatrick,
Sanders, and Worthen 2004): Formative evaluation is what's happening
when a cook tastes a soup and adds salt, then tastes it a few minutes later
and adds basil. Summative evaluation is what's happening when a restau-

rant patron tastes the soup after it's served and either smiles or grimaces. Both types of evaluation are important when dealing with educational products, but we have more interest in *building* those products than in looking back on them once they're done. Therefore, we'll focus on how formative evaluation ameliorates ILOs and promotes micro-collaboration.

Formative evaluation is the linchpin of iterative development, insofar as iterative development calls on the team to continuously revise the ILO, even as it's being built. This results in a deliverable that, nine times out of ten, coincides with or surpasses the team's original vision. Thus, we have reason to consider formative evaluation the primary advantage of iterative development. It is the interstitial phase that makes each iteration of the deliverable better than its predecessor. If formative evaluation didn't yield results, iterative development wouldn't work, and as we saw in chapter 4, it *does* work.

In this chapter, we'll argue that because formative evaluation is so essential to iterative development, it ought to be *formalized*. Formalization ensures that each iteration of the deliverable comes closer to achieving the team's long-term goals. In other words, formalization helps the team use formative evaluation to the greatest possible benefit. To make our case, we'll delve into the contributions of formative evaluation, and propose some formalization tools.

Elaboration on Evaluation

Evaluative methods are a mainstay of academic culture. This is especially true in so-called research institutions, which favor evaluative protocols associated with empirical evidence. These research-based protocols are largely homologous with those by which we conduct formative evaluation. The main difference between them is intent: while both research and evaluation strive for impartiality, the purpose of the former is mainly to test theories, whereas the purpose of the latter is mainly to back up claims, assess efficiencies, or contribute to a continuous improvement program.

It should go without saying that evaluations conducted by an ILO team will be a far cry from research conducted by, for instance, a federally funded team of physicists working with a multi-million dollar particle accelerator. Trying to make them identical would be more amusing than productive, and completely beside the point. Formative evaluation is useful to ILO teams because by performing controlled user-tests and applying the results, the team can adjust its idea of what works, recalibrate its efforts, and come closer to solving its central problem: how to communicate tacit knowledge from the instructor-expert to the deliverable.

Unlike their counterparts in academia, ILO teams working in the private sector (and in associations or nonprofits) are often left without the resources to conduct formative evaluation, except in the most informal ways. The development process is either (1) bid out, with formative evaluation being sacrificed in the name of a low budget, or (2) heaped on an overworked department for which rapidity trumps all else. When upper-level (i.e., program) management makes formative evaluation all but impossible, it stands to reason that the deliverable will not reach its full potential. Unfortunately, this state of affairs tends to leave private-sector project managers with little recourse; as we noted in chapter 4, project managers need to work within whatever constraints are imposed on the project by outside forces. Upper-level managers *can*, of course, be *convinced* of the urgent need for formative evaluation, with which the current chapter will help.

The sheer cost of developing ILOs constitutes a strong implicit argument in support of formative evaluation. Universities and corporations pour hundreds of thousands of dollars into eLearning products. Investments of that magnitude need to be rewarded with the highest quality returns, and common sense tells us that formative evaluation leads to such returns—how, indeed, could it not? By describing learners' needs ever more precisely, formative evaluation sets a direction for the ILO team, one that will bring them to the most effective and sophisticated deliverable possible (allowing for the limitations of the triple constraint).

In addition to this common-sense conclusion, researchers like Tessmer inform us that "over the last 30 years, a number of empirical studies have shown that formatively evaluating instructional materials has resulted in revised instruction that produces statistically significant increases in student performance over the original, unevaluated versions of the instruction" (Tessmer 2002). According to Barbara Flagg, author of *Formative Evaluation of Educational Technologies*, the information accumulated through formative evaluation is applicable to three broad categories of ILO development: decisions, objectives, and public relations (Flagg 1990). To put it more specifically, formative evaluation answers the following: What sort of features should we program into the deliverable? What does the deliverable actually do for learners? What's the best way to promote the deliverable to its target audience?

Furthermore, formative evaluation has a catalytic effect on micro-collaboration; it mobilizes and energizes the team, drawing out new ideas and unveiling new paths to explore (Chacon-Moscoso et al. 2002). It can even jump-start the instructor-expert's natural inclination to learn more about his or her subject area. As a stage of the development process, it establishes a forum/avenue for micro-collaborative communication.

Formalization

We see, then, that ILO development preponderates with reasons to use formative evaluation. That being so, doesn't it make sense for formative evaluation be made a *formal* aspect of the team's working process?

It's not that formality is strictly necessary. A team can glean some benefit from formative evaluation simply by chatting with a user after he or she tries an iteration. As Tessmer writes, "formative evaluation is deceptively easy to conduct, since one can simply grab a learner or an expert to 'look over the instruction'" (2001). Perhaps the project's budget is so attenuated by program-level factors that this bare-minimum approach is the only option. That's fine: it's better than nothing, and *will* have a positive effect on the deliverable.

It will *not*, unfortunately, meet the full potential of formative evaluation. Based on both research and personal experience in private practice,

Figure 17. User testing of an ILO for the World Anti-Doping Agency (this ILO was built using a rewritable dialogue engine, which allowed for efficient modifications following user tests in multiple cultures). © 2010 WADA.

it's abundantly clear that when formative evaluation is *formalized*, it amplifies an ILO team's momentum and product-improvement efforts. This is especially true in the case of instructor-experts. Formative evaluation tends to increase instructor-experts' personal investment in the deliverable. It's easy to pick up on instructor-experts' sense of accomplishment and enthusiasm during formal formative evaluation: standing in a classroom, watching learners test a version of the ILO, it dawns on them just how great the deliverable could be, and they start planning ways to get there.]

According to Tessmer, "The most effective evaluations begin with an evaluation plan ... [The plan should] specify evaluation subjects, information goals, questions, data gathering tools, and the review and revision process" (2001). Tessmer's checklist suggests that managers answer the following questions (2001, with slight revisions made for readability):

1. Who will make evaluation decisions?

2. What are the deadlines for evaluation decisions?

3. What are the goals of the evaluation?

4. What personnel and resources are available for the evaluation?

5. What are the constraints on the scope/duration of the evaluation?

6. What will be learned via task analysis?

7. Should learning or work performance be assessed?

8. What environmental aspects can affect learning?

9. What instructor characteristics may affect implementation?

10. What media attributes should be evaluated?

11. In what stages will the evaluation take place?

12. Who will be used: Experts? Learners? Administrators? Instructors?

13. When will each stage be conducted/completed?

14. What data gathering tools and procedures will be used?

15. What information will go into the evaluation report?

16. Who will see the evaluation report?

When the answers to these questions are incorporated into the team's articulation documents and distributed to everyone involved, formative evaluation is pushed to the next level—and so, by extension, is the ILO.

Program-level Evaluation

The Engage program—which houses not only Cool-It, but various other ILOs created through UW-Madison's Department of Instructional Technology—conducts formal evaluations on a yearly basis. These cover the program as a whole, and are used to communicate accomplishments, pitfalls, and funding needs to the advisory board. By using formal evaluation methods to identify what works and what doesn't, Engage is able to document where investments will be most effective.

What's more, Engage used its years' worth of evaluation data to develop an EduCause workshop called GAMEQUEST. Created by both management and staff, Game Quest highlighted roadblocks and outright failures experienced by Engage projects, both former and ongoing, so as to help everyone learn from them. During impromptu gatherings and brown-bag lunch sessions, it was apparent that Engage's program-level evaluations were successful in prompting reflection, discussion, and plans for change.

Formative Evaluation
During Cool-It's Development

The Engage program's emphasis on evaluation naturally influenced the Cool-It team. For one thing, Engage management insisted that evaluation materials be posted to the program website. For another, Engage hired an internal evaluator, Lindsay Schmidt, to assist teams in setting up their evaluation protocols. The Cool-It Wiki contains artifacts of their meetings (University of Wisconsin-Madison 2011c).

As the program-level evaluation coordinator, Schmidt did not conduct user tests for each of Cool-It's iterations. That fell to production assistant Chris Blakesley, who recalls,

> With Cool-It, I was assigned to lead user testing because I was in school, and doing research was the name of the game ... I tended to be the meticulous person when it came to formulating questions and protocol, and we also had a book resource we drew from. Dave would [use a more intuitive approach] to get at the questions he was interested in. He'd ask things like, 'What did

you learn from this?' or 'Why was this one thing tricky?' But it was structured [formally], such that someone would observe and introduce it all and help [the students].

Blakesley says that the team would take notes on the results of user testing and review them over the course of the next meeting. "So typically what happened," says Pfotenhauer, "was that Dave and Mike would come back from the user testing and share with the rest of us, 'Here's what we found while they were doing it.' And again, it was usually very exciting because this was brand new. [We] had no idea how the students were going to behave with it. And so... Dave and Mike would describe: 'Well this is what they did, and they suggested *this*.' And we all went, 'Oh yeah, what a cool idea.' So there's one feature in the game that has this interactive graphing tool, and that was an outcome of the user testing. That was a great idea."

Initially, Cool-It's user testing was based on learners' responses to whiteboard drawings and rudimentary graphics. This was in keeping with Les Howles's commitment to "only increas[ing] the fidelity of the prototype as early as you need to." Gagnon knew that even if users didn't entirely comprehend what they were looking at, especially when it came to the esoteric cryogenics subject-matter, they could describe the process by which they were attempting to unravel it. Understanding that process was important for designing instructional activities.

Hence, formative evaluation can be productive at even the earliest stages. By soliciting learners' reactions to rough, ultra-cheap mockups, the Cool-It team was able to make informed decisions when it came to designing expensive prototypical iterations, and, by the same token, was able to avoid sinking resources into unwieldy or ineffective trial runs.

That said, formative evaluation will yield the most dramatic results when users have something a little more weighty to evaluate. Litzkow admits that he prefers to user-test working prototypes, rather than paper printouts or whiteboard hypotheticals.

"At a certain point in the development process," recalls Litzkow, "I was able to come up with a new, updated version almost every week. We were able to sit down as a team and talk to the [instructor-expert] to figure out, for example, whether the meters were going the right way. [So I find that] having a physical programming artifact that you can actually interact with makes things very clear to the instructor-expert ... the instructor-expert and the students really don't get what the game is like until that point."

The Problem with Informality

Formative evaluation must verify not only that users understand how the activity works, but also that the activities are aligned with the learning objectives. ILO teams do not set out to create games and simulations purely for entertainment value—as mentioned in chapter 2, there are plenty of hundred-million-dollar enterprises whose sole aim is entertainment. Rather, ILO teams set out to achieve specific educational goals. This needs to be reflected in their formative evaluation procedures.

The Engage program has a very strong culture of evaluation. It emphasizes innovation and exploration, accepting that occasional inefficiencies are the price of discovery. Innovation and exploration are indeed good things, but unfortunately, they're sometimes seen as antithetical to formalization. Accordingly, the Cool-It team's formative evaluations were informal. The problem with informal formative evaluation is that it doesn't usually call for specific design features to be in place for specific user tests. Therefore, user tests cannot be tailored in advance to each version of the deliverable. The tests are not made to address *particular* aspects of the deliverable—or, if they are made that way, they may not coincide with when those aspects are actually programmed into the deliverable. Essentially, when a team uses informal formative evaluation, its evaluation timeline is likely to be out of step with its iterative design timeline. This can lead to some design mechanics never being evaluated properly. These mechanics fly under the radar, their alignment with learning objectives never being called into question.

By contrast, a *formal* formative evaluation plan calls for specific design mechanics to be in place by specific dates. It matches the iterative design timeline with the evaluation timeline. That way, user tests can be tailored to address the mechanics that the team needs to work on. The idea here is to maintain a level of scientific control over user testing: make sure it's addressing the right features, and make sure it's reflective of the team's long-term goal of aligning activates with learning outcomes.

Overview

The iterative development process, which is so well suited to ILOs, draws much of its strength from formative evaluation. If iterative development is the map of an ILO's creation, then formative evaluation traces the *route* the team takes to get from start to finish. The route needs to match up with the map—otherwise, the team will waste resources on wrong turns and dead ends.

If you'll permit us to strain the metaphor, we'll say that informal formative evaluation is like trying to drive across the US using a collection of taped-together local maps that only show the back roads. You *might* get to your destination, and you might even see interesting things along the way, but it'll take a lot longer, you'll spend more on gas, and your maps will be of limited value. Using formal formative evaluation, on the other hand, is like driving across the US using dedicated map of the interstate: you know where you want to go, you plan your route in advance, you know all your stops, and you keep your eye on the final destination.

Thus, formalizing formative evaluation is the best way to ensure that every iteration of the deliverable is a step *forward*, rather than sideways or backwards—a step that coincides with the team's priorities and takes the deliverable closer to its ideal state. In the next chapter, we'll build on this argument by discussing how to combine the right *direction* with the necessary *impetus*, or momentum.

<<MICRO-COLLABORATION IN PRACTICE>>
By Jon Aleckson with Richard Schafer
BlueKids: Formative Evaluation and the Business Model

Since 2004, the Children's Health Education Center (CHEC) of the Children's Hospital of Wisconsin has been using game-based online learning objects to teach grade- and middle-school students about such things as obesity, bullying, and ATOD prevention. CHEC uses the sort of LMS / content-management system you'd find in higher education; the content-management system acts as a "container" for fourteen curriculums. Known collectively as "BlueKids," each container holds about ten ILOs, any one of which can be introduced over a three- to eight-week period. All told, CHEC provides teachers with fourteen extensive curriculums; every curriculum is accompanied by a guide that outlines multiples ways of introducing the ILOs and integrating them with other forms of classroom instruction. BlueKids programs are offered via a blended approach, with students engaged in five to six eLearning lessons combined with five to six teacher-led discussions; this gives teachers the chance to personalize the lessons based on the local community and the school's needs.

The use of a branded BlueKids LMS enables CHEC to collect user data during and after development. CHEC includes both teachers and students in its reviews and user testing; the organization implements detailed evaluation plans (both formative and summative) that include input from all stakeholders. It's one of the reasons BlueKids has been so successful—BlueKids reached 43,000 learners in the 2010-2011 school year.

Dr. Richard Schafer, Manager of CHEC BlueKids eLearning development and research efforts, describes the curriculum-development cycle in terms of formative evaluation. The pre-development phase consists mainly of research and analysis pertaining to the health topic in question; findings are supplemented with feedback from educators, who speak to the depth and grade-appropriateness of the proposed content and learning activities. Stakeholder input comes from focus groups that respond to content outlines, conceptual diagrams of learning activities, and samples of screen art.

Once the team moves into the development phase, it progresses in stages: Prototype (crude storyboards), Alpha, Beta, Pilot, and Final. Actual user testing starts at the Beta stage.

According to Schafer, a team wants to answer the following questions as early as possible:

1. Does the subject matter resonate with the learners?

2. Is the level of learning too difficult from teachers' or students' perspective?

3. Do the student testers like and relate to the art/characters within the story?

4. Is the graphic interface easy to use?

5. Do learners *enjoy* the games? Are teachers satisfied with the games' assessment components?

6. Is the pacing of the activities appropriate—neither too fast nor too slow?

7. Do teachers feel the program will be easy to implement in the classroom?

8. Do teachers relate to the learning objectives and learning outcomes?

"So for example," says Schafer, "we found during user testing of our latest program, 'The Great Safety Adventure,' that the animations and voice balloons left the screen to rapidly. Teachers and students were all saying, 'They disappeared before we could read them.' And we also learned—this was through user testing of our middle school ACT NOW Bully Program—that trying to save money by including PDF reading assignments just doesn't work. Students had no interest in reading the PDFs. They were far more likely to watch a video and answer questions about it."

CHEC staff and the development company they work with are always running a kind of formative evaluation triage: they comb through electronic surveys and users' comments to highlight the deliverable's most important issues. Says Schafer, "Using surveys and other types of written documentation, as well as holding meetings with development staff—it keeps stakeholders focused. It helps make sure we're investing resources in the most important things. Budgets are always tight, and you have to

Figure 18. The main menu of a CHEC online game-based learning program. Learners receive assignments via a virtual phone and keep notes in a journal as they visit various locations in town in order to help solve a major puzzle by interviewing residents. © 2010 Children's Hospital of Wisconsin.

make negotiations and compromises at every stage, with the goal being to use your limited resources in the most effective way, so that you're getting a great learning activity within your budget and within your timeframe. What upper management keeps in mind is that each iteration is just that: it's a version, and you have to re-invest in it based on user feedback. Not just once, but as part of an ongoing process."

CHEC runs a tight eighteen-week development cycle for every curriculum project. An iteration lands in front of users by week six, is refined by week twelve, and is piloted in a full classroom by week sixteen. The cycle coincides with the fall and spring semesters; after the first semester's exposure, it goes back to development to be revised according to teachers' and students' suggestions. "What we ask the teachers," says Schafer, "is, 'If you're going to implement this in the classroom, what type of learner outcomes do you expect?' One of the critical success factors of user testing is to get the testers to focus on, 'Wow. What can we do to make this better?'

> And one of the things that makes it far more likely for you to get *future* access to user testers is if you *show* them how their feedback matters. You show them the action-item lists or the changes you've made in an iteration. You basically just treat them with dignity and respect, and let them know that their time is really worth something to you. What we do is try to give students and teachers a token of thanks, like a gift card for a local restaurant. Because their input is hugely important.

A formative evaluation plan, in combination with summative evaluation, is an important piece of a program's business model. It speaks to financial sustainability. In the beginning, CHEC *thought* it knew how to sell teachers on using its ILOs, but things didn't go as expected. CHEC's current, highly successful business plan was built on trial, error, and revision—all of which paid off in the end, as CHEC reaches 70% more students with each passing school year. According to Schafer, one of the keys to CHEC's success is its ability to provide school district personnel with concrete data. "We can empirically prove, based on our evaluations, that our programs make a difference when it comes to student behavior, student attitude—it's more than just content acquisition. Having that empirical proof is key if you want your program to grow, to be universally accepted, and to be financially successful. Decision makers love data and we have the numbers to back up our claims. That's another thing our evaluation practices have done for us."

CHAPTER 7

Momentum: The Panoramic Factor

> What often separates extraordinary projects from
> adequate projects is the team's enthusiasm. When you
> have enthusiasm you have cohesion, and that makes for a
> good end product. But the team can't just hope
> enthusiasm comes upon them magically. Everyone needs
> to take responsibility for creating those high-energy
> moments—like prepping for a formal conference
> presentation—in which people are rediscovering their
> passion and moving forward with new resolve.
> —*Kurt Squire, UW-Madison*

Personal momentum is a difficult thing to measure, at least in the quantitative sense. There is no laboratory instrument capable of detecting it; no scale with which to express its magnitude; no unit in which to write its volume, density, or mass. Unlike the inertia of Newtonian matter, personal momentum isn't subject to a formula. It's fickle. It's frustrating as often as it's energizing. In addressing it, we may be forced to lean on vague semantic formulas rather than empirical data, and this makes us hesitant to address it at all: what can we say about momentum that will be backed up in the traditional academic ways, by theorists or social scientists who track percentages and concrete outcomes? How do we track what is instead a combination of senses—the sense of urgency and the sense of enthusiasm?

Various people have come up with answers of varying merit, but frankly, we're not interested in an empirical record of momentum. This is a book about practice, and it seems sensible, therefore, to make a straightforward appeal to common experience. Hasn't almost everyone felt, at one point or another, the dramatic difference between doing something with momentum and doing the same thing without? Projects go through high points and low points; at the high points, things just seem to flow. Graduate students writing their dissertations, entry-level employees formatting business reports, professors demonstrating lab experiments, business executives hashing out deals in boardrooms—no matter your field, no matter your place in the pecking order, momentum affects how you go about your day to day tasks.

The truth is that momentum—although difficult to describe in exactly the same way as, for instance, video game mechanics—is not some occult mystery. It's actually quite familiar. It can be managed similarly to the other factors, even if we tend to talk about it differently.

As you may recall, our five factor model for enabling micro-collaboration on ILO projects places momentum at the center of the other four factors:

In this chapter, we'll revisit the theoretical underpinnings of our model and discuss momentum's peculiar relation to the factors that sur-

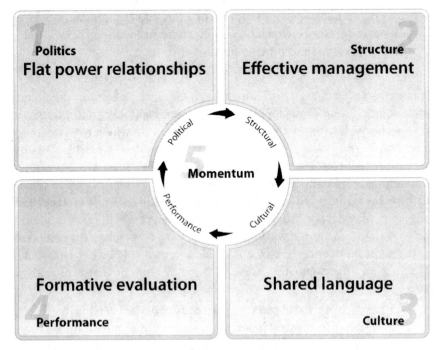

Figure 19: Aleckson's five factors of micro-collaboration.

round it. This will lead us to a review of the material in the preceding chapters, including some aspects of the Cool-It story in which momentum is salient. At the end we'll provide a list of tips on how to spike momentum when it wanes.

Frames and Dimensions

In chapter 1, we provided a brief explanation of the schema proposed by Bolman and Deal in *Reframing Organizations: Artistry, Choice, and Leadership*. Bolman and Deal identify four frames: structural, human resource, political, and symbolic (2008). Each frame represents a unique way of understanding an organization; in effect, each is an interpretive strategy. Each tells us something important, but none tells us *everything*. To really figure out how an organization works, we need to be able to see it through each individual frame and to *synthesize* the information that each frame yields into a coherent whole.

Samuel Bacharach also establishes a four-part model, though he zeroes in on momentum and the dimensions through which it can be manipulated by proactive managers; these dimensions include the performance, cultural, structural, and political (2006). For Bacharach, momentum is one of the decisive differences between good ideas that are executed and good ideas that languish or expire:

> It is easy to underestimate the difficulties that stand in the way of putting ideas in place. The tendency is to think that a good idea will carry the day; but it simply won't … Because interests are often entrenched, hesitation and resistance may be a stronger force than a good idea. Inertia is the name of the game [and managing momentum is how proactive leaders get inertia to work in their favor]. (Bacharach 2006)

For most part, Bacharach addresses "leaders," whom we tend to think of as people with the authority to make project-, program-, or department-level decisions. This obviously resonates with some of what we have to say, especially our chapter on project management. However, we afford equal attention to other members of the project team, members who may not have a leadership role but still have a huge impact on micro-collaboration.

Indeed, our model treats micro-collaboration in much the way that Bacharach's treats momentum. He gives momentum pride of place: it is one of the key factors—if not *the* key factor—that leaders need to manipulate if they're going to accomplish their goals. As he writes, "Sustaining momentum is the litmus test of managerial competence" (Bacharach 2006). We, on the other hand, give that place over to micro-collaboration (which lets us put less emphasis on leadership per se, even though leadership is clearly of great importance to project momentum). Although we acknowledge momentum's influence over micro-collaboration, we treat it as one of Bolman and Deal's frames: it is but one perspective from which to view micro-collaboration. Crucial, yes, but not more crucial or more basic than the other four factors.

How Momentum Manifests

We've already brought up that momentum isn't quite the same as the other factors. That's why it doesn't have its own, solid frame in our model, but occupies the empty area at the center. This area (someone in the contemporary art world might call it "negative space") is delineated by the first four factors in such a way that if we removed any of them, the area would lose its shape. It would become undefined.

Just so, the lived experience of momentum takes its meaning from other, more concrete aspects of our work. We understand it as a characteristic that may or may not be present while we're programming code, composing an article for peer review, or meeting with shareholders. It is, as we've said before, dynamic. When we step into the momentum space, we don't see solid objects to describe. The space is only "visible" in the presence of the other four factors. Therefore, if we're going to talk about momentum, we'll do best to talk about how it's *instantiated*.

The point to which we're building here is that the way to maintain positive momentum on ILO projects is, quite simply, to follow our advice regarding the other four factors. If you flatten power relationships, establish a dedicated project management position / use an iterative design process, take advantage of communication strategies to establish a shared language, and formalize formative evaluation, then your project's momentum is going to work in your favor.

By way of elaboration, we'll break down momentum along the same lines as Bacharach, starting with the point that requires the most explication.

Political. The term "political" is sometimes associated with cutthroat or Machiavellian strategic maneuvering. Such maneuvering is standard operating procedure in the vast majority of organizations; unfortunately, it subtly encourages us to think of people in a utilitarian or mechanistic way, to the point that even our recognition of their talents/capabilities is carefully calculated. In other words, we end up thinking of people as chess pieces. When we're seeing things in that light, people not in leadership positions are usually relegated to the status of pawns.

Is it sometimes useful to think that way? Yes; political maneuvering is a vital skill in both the academic and business worlds. Pretending otherwise would be naïve.

However, when it comes to micro-collaboration on ILO projects, maintaining political momentum entails *flattening power relationships*, and as we discussed in chapter 3, one of the deeply ingrained habits that makes it difficult to flatten power relationships is the tendency of some instructor-experts (especially in academia) to think of the IDD team as ... well, as pawns. As low-level functionaries that serve a purpose without having any exceptional abilities—without, that is, having much in the way of expertise. It's not a universal attitude by far, but it's around. (In some cases, it's reflected in the way funds are allocated: who controls the money for ILO projects? The IT department? The ILO program? Or some other arm of the organization?) Encouraging a different mindset is one of the most important aspects of infusing the ILO with the instructor-expert's tacit knowledge and thus accomplishing the team's learning objectives.

Therefore, maintaining political momentum on ILO projects means moving away from the utilitarian or mechanistic character of intra-organizational politics, which often—though not necessarily—downplays the particular genius of people in non-leadership positions. We're not saying that that type of intra-organizational politics can be ignored, but it should *inflect* the politics of ILO design and development as little as possible. It will be important for anyone in any organization to maintain a tactical awareness of the political landscape, but the best way to exercise this awareness during an ILO initiative is to make sure that *everyone's* contributions are regarded as essential.

(Bacharach's not at all oblivious to this necessity; he even has a section labeled "Create Hierarchies but Don't Forget Teams," which he places in the structural dimension [2006]. Our point is that flattening power relationships is *the* thrust of our political frame.)

Politically, the Cool-It team was exemplary; reproducing a few quotes from chapter 3 should be ample proof.

From programmer Mike Litzkow: "It is important to start off early with the idea that this is teamwork. It takes people with diverse talents to put together a good game [that is, ILO]. The [instructor-expert] is essential, but they are not in charge ... They need to look at other individuals as on a level playing field."

From instructor-expert John Pfotenhauer: "We have a real good balance of lots of different expertise. I have the expertise of the content, but it's very obvious that, you know, there are others, like Mike Litzkow, who has the expertise about how to make the programming happen, and the animators, to add features. And frankly, David has the expertise of knowing how to make it game-like, so that it's beyond just a simulator that makes you calculate things easily."

When you flatten power relationships and respect the contributions of the IDD team, positive political momentum will follow.

Structural. For us, structural momentum is the province of project management. Recall our discussion of the triple constraint: schedule, scope, and cost. A hitch in any of these areas can cause a precipitous drop in momentum, and it's up to a project manager to minimize those hitches. This amount of responsibility means that project managers should not have to play any other role; they should not, for instance, have to be instructional designers as well as project managers. Splitting roles can create conflicts of interest (opportunities for innovative or exciting designs must be sacrificed due to budget, etc.), disorient the team, and ultimately reduce momentum.

One of the best things a project manager (or program manager, depending on how the organization is set up) can do is implement an iterative design paradigm—Agile or some variation thereof.

Iterative design gives an ILO project the best chance of meeting learners' needs while still coming in on time, on spec, and on budget. It keeps the team from sinking resources into a deliverable that won't accomplish its learning objects and gives team members plenty of chances for reflection-in-action, which in turn contributes to their professional development and the flattening of power relationships. Because of its mechanics, iterative development makes the most of micro-collaboration.

However, because of those same mechanics, iterative development requires strong project management. Iterative development provides team members with so many options as to how to direct their energy that their energy is at risk of becoming hopelessly diffuse. It's up to the project manager to focus the team's efforts on the most pressing or relevant of the deliverable's problems. (As noted, it is in this frame that Bacharach's attention to leadership translates most readily to ILOs.)

We saw that Cool-It employed its own version of iterative design but ran into issues with regard to project management. Budget- and time-wise, Cool-It's numbers were higher than intended. Did this completely kill the team's enthusiasm? No. But a certain dampening was both predictable and perceptible in interviews: "You know, you can entertain the idea of accelerating the process by having meetings more often and trying, in between the meetings, to get more work done for the game," said Pfotenhauer. "If I was starting over . . . I would consider [ways to accelerate things], just in view of how long it takes to get something done, [even though I was pleased with what we accomplished.]"

Cultural. We see cultural momentum as being all about communication—that is, about establishing a shared language between all stakeholders in the ILO. Sophisticated ILOs rely heavily on narrative to accomplish their educational goals. In order for narrative to be effective, as opposed to merely entertaining, it needs to be grounded in the real-life experiences of the instructor-expert. It is only through such grounding that the instructor-expert's tacit knowledge can be imparted to the learner.

Immersing the learner as thoroughly as possible in the instructor-expert's world—said immersion being what teaches learners to *think as* experts, as opposed to simply mimicking experts—requires all members of the ILO development team to feel personally invested in the project. They need to (1) feel comfortable relating anecdotes from their own lives and (2) be able to distinguish between anecdotes that are germane to the project or meeting and anecdotes that ought to be saved for some other time.

That crucial blend of comfort and discernment can be cultivated by using the proper meeting artifacts, especially visualization tools. It can also be cultivated through discussing the theoretical aspects of ILO design, including the relationship of videogames to situated learning/pedagogy. The goal here is to create a *common vision* of the deliverable.

As we saw, the Cool-It team had an enviable rapport. They used both their personal experiences and various visualization tools to make the realities of the cryogenics lab a foundational aspect of the ILO, even as they cut down on unpalatable didactic elements. Their micro-collaborative communication kept them enthusiastic—that is, highly motivated—during all stages of the project, even those that started off seeming forbiddingly abstruse or maddeningly technical. They were able to relate their close-in, highly detailed, and occasionally frustrating tasks to an exciting and worthwhile common goal, which kept their morale from bottoming out when things didn't happen on schedule (something with which we are all doubtless familiar).

Performance. Performance momentum involves using formative evaluation to monitor the team's progress and make sure the deliverable is constantly improving. Naturally, the quality of the team's formative evaluations has a dramatic effect on the efficiency of its iterative design process. Formative evaluations determine how each version of the deliverable will differ from its predecessor; therefore, formative evaluations are responsible for nudging the deliverable either closer or farther from its ideal form. When formative evaluations are conducted informally, they are at risk of being dominated by short-term thinking, which can lead to important evaluative criteria being overlooked or deferred for too long (cf. our discussion of Cool-It's formative evaluations in chapter 6). *Formalizing* formative evaluation is a way of ensuring that the ILO's design features undergo continuous improvement, and that short-term iterative revisions are in line with the team's long-term goals.

Formal formative evaluations prompt all team members to reflect on their skill sets and critique their own contributions to the deliverable; accordingly, they provide an excellent forum for communication. They can also get the instructor-expert more actively involved in the project: when he or she sees concrete changes being made based on his or her suggestions, and, on top of that, has the chance to watch learners using prototypes of the ILO, then he or she tends to feel more connected to the end product, more invested in its quality.

Paying formal attention to the team's performance via user-testing protocols amplifies momentum by sparking communication and highlighting forward progress.

Momentum-specific Strategies and Overview

The danger of separating momentum from the other factors is that when we talk about it, we can get bogged down in vague descriptions (and, it's fair to say, convoluted metaphors). The solution? Our prized practical experience with ILOs. The following list takes the above discussion and reformulates it as straightforward, down-to-earth suggestions for spiking a team's momentum before, during, and after a specific ILO project (we've also added some heretofore unmentioned points). Many of these items will hinge on the project/program manager, but it's a good idea for all team members to be aware of them and, if necessary, bring them up.

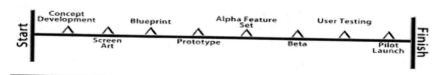

Figure 20. Spiking momentum.

Pre-development Stage

Benchmarking and theorizing. Find similar online learning activities (exemplars) and get everyone (including the instructor-expert) involved in discussing why some of them are successful as learning tools and some aren't. Don't leave it up to the instructor-expert to write learning objectives—most won't have experience writing objectives for online education, so it will be useful to have the IDD team involved. Make this meeting fun!

Artwork introduction. Organize strategic presentations of everything from pencil-drawn stick figures to professional art, and get input from everyone. Not only is high-quality art a solid investment for ILOs; experience also tells us that people's enthusiasm jumps when new visuals are revealed.

Prototyping. Programming concepts should be roughly demonstrated early on to convince the instructor-expert of the IDD team's competency and individuals' ability to achieve their goals. Working prototypes engage stakeholders. They increase everyone's vim and verve.

User-testing reflection. This is a good way of reminding everyone that ILOs are all about the learner. On a related note, finding a few novice user-testers can serve to remind the expert of what it was like to learn the material from an uninitiated perspective. Watching learners experience the ILO tends to be a "goosebumps moment" for stakeholders.

Development Stage

Presentations. When the IDD team comes up with new iterations, it has to present them to the instructor-expert with some panache, some showmanship. IDD team members too often assume that the instructor expert will be brimming with enthusiasm right from the start, which isn't usually the case: the instructor-expert often needs to be *sold* on the project. Don't just send him or her a link to the ILO. Make it engaging, make it convincing. Instead of relying on enthusiasm, *create* it.

Pace the introduction of traditionally exciting material. Art-based character development or the selection of voice talent can be broken into time-spaced events to drive interest and enthusiasm. In other words: give people something to look forward to. This requires forethought in the early stages. (Keep in mind that some instructor-experts won't want to participate in every one of these events-if you're on the IDD team, don't get hung up on it, even though it's best for the ILO if the instructor-expert is involved in all major milestones.)

Formative evaluation. Make it a responsibility of the instructor-expert to round up user-testers and participate in crafting questions to elicit actionable user responses. (A tip: online user-testing services allow for video recordings of users experimenting with the ILO.)

Post-development Stage

Iterative culture. All team members, including the instructor-expert, should keep in mind that the "final" version of the deliverable is not immutable. Even after the initial deadline has passed, the ILO is a work in progress. This understanding should actually be established in the pre-development stage, but it has the greatest ramifications for momentum in the post-development stage.

Summative version evaluations. These should be scheduled periodically and include reflective sessions on how the ILO could be (or could have been) made better. Same for the development process itself.

Awards. Enter the ILO into contests. Encourage people to take pride in it.

Conference submissions. Assist the instructor-expert in organizing and writing an article or presentation on the ILO project.

Plan for the next one. There will always be more to do, and sometimes, ideas that didn't fit into the first version of the ILO can be incorporated into redesigns or used to enhance new projects, so keep a list of "Version 2.0 features."

Overview

The purposes of this chapter have been to (1) clarify how the momentum factor is instantiated within ILO teams and (2) revisit a few important points from chapters 3 through 6. We've made repeated reference to Bacharach's dimensions of momentum because as a general outline, his model corresponds conveniently to ours. It's a useful reminder of how our first four factors both shape and are shaped by momentum, such that each one's relationship to momentum can be thought of as a feedback loop.

We've also reviewed the Cool-It story, and what we've seen is a team of highly skilled and dedicated professionals who did almost everything right. If certain aspects of their story are criticizable, then they simply demonstrate that even the very competent can benefit from the study of micro-collaboration.

To summarize: When you move into the momentum frame, you acquire a 360-degree panoramic view of the other four factors. In other words, you're looking *outward*. If you find that something's wrong with momentum, it probably means that something is going wrong in the area of power relationships, project management, communication, or formal evaluation. The problem might not be visible from *within* the factor (or frame), but all too clear once you've acquired a little distance from it by stepping into momentum. That's why we've extracted momentum from the other factors and placed it at the hub or nexus of our model. Thinking of momentum as a fifth frame of reference makes it easier to assess an ILO team's status *holistically*; by the same token, monitoring momentum and employing the strategies listed above will help improve the team's grade in *every* factor.

<<MICRO-COLLABORATION IN PRACTICE>>

By Penny Ralston-Berg with Meg Gaines and Sarah Davis
Center for Patient Partnerships, Komen for the Cure, Madison Affiliate

The Komen Self-Advocacy Project gives patients facing cancer a way to educate themselves on how to shape their own health care. In addition to providing key knowledge and support, the project teaches concrete skills that can come into play at critical health care junctures. The skills in question relate not only to physical health, but also to paying for care, maintaining employment, and sustaining emotional wellbeing.

In creating an ILO for the Komen Project, we built up a kind of natural momentum right from the beginning, and this momentum facilitated our micro-collaboration and sustained us all the way through the end. Our ultimate goal was to take the knowledge and information provided by the Center and translate it in two fundamental ways. First, the starting content was a curriculum that taught advocates to work with patients, and we had to make it a curriculum for self-advocacy. Second, the content started off in face-to-face format, and we were making an eLearning product out of it.

When it came to both these goals, the enthusiasm of the instructor-experts-Meg Gaines and Sarah Davis-was contagious from the very first meeting. Their passion and genuine wish to help others was unmistakable and had a big impact on the team as a whole. Coming in as a designer, I found myself energized by meeting with them. I acquired a strong sense of personal connection to the project. On top of this, Davis tells me that "working with an instructional designer brought new eyes to the whole endeavor and infused everyone with a new energy. We had of course pitched the project to our funders because we thought it was a good idea and we believed in it, but having an expert in adult learning theory, someone who doesn't work in our field day in and day out-having that person come in and say, 'Wow, this is great, and it's going to be incredible,' was extremely motivating."

I find that at the start of a project it's important to hear the goals from the source-that is, from the people who are running the project, who dreamed it up in the first place. You have to take the time to listen, to take in their passion and figure out why the project is important to them. Why did they write a grant or propose a new course or program? How did they get to the point of hiring a designer? There always comes a time to ask about audience, learning objectives, and the specifics of instruction. But before any of that there is an opportunity to listen, observe, and connect-to become attached and invested in someone else's idea. Having that shared passion acts as a motivating factor that persists throughout the entire project. I felt this type of connection and motivation with Gaines and Davis.

After the instructor-experts related the project's backstory, we talked about how they expected learners to interact with each other, how they expected learners to interact with the materials, how the materials would be used, and what they expected the learners to get out of the training. These were not lesson-specific objectives but rather overarching goals. Sharing overarching goals at the start of a project will help set experts and designers on the same path, the same mission. Once the ultimate goals are spelled out, it's easier to work toward them in synchrony.

Design Plan

As we discussed the flow of activities and our plan for how learning would take place, we also considered the technologies that would be used to deliver the materials. There was the potential for an exceptionally high-level ILO; specifically, an opportunity for learners to interact with virtual patients who presented their cases and feelings through an avatar. Using intelligent agents, the learner could ask questions of the virtual patients to gather more information about the case.

This method of delivery, although intriguing to the instructor-experts, was more than what was appropriate for their pilot audience and the scope of their grant. The number of production hours required to develop such a complex ILO did not match the grant funds and was not commensurate with the computer savvy of their pilot group. We decided that a visually appealing text and case-based format would be better.

Nevertheless, our ideas for a more complex ILO weren't abandoned. The content was designed so as to be convertible to more interactive formats as the project is shared and the audience continues to grow. We also included photos and audio excerpts from real cases to draw the audience in. Knowing that the ILO could would become better and better in future versions helped us maintain our enthusiasm for the first version.

Ultimately, what led to the ILO being simultaneously on spec and highly versatile was the team's energy: because we cared, we poured a lot of effort and emotion into getting it exactly right. By sharing our perspectives and our skills, we shared our passion for the project, which in turn reinforced everyone's momentum and benefited our learners.

Afterword

Whether in business or academia, the value of any pedagogical tool is measured by its effect on its intended audience: do the people using it learn what they're supposed to? Having used the tool, are they more skilled, more knowledgeable, more capable of completing the tasks set before them?

If supervisors and professors want to answer Yes to those questions (and why wouldn't they?), then they'll probably end up presenting students/employees—i.e., learners—with some type of *bricolage*: a half-improvised collection of hands-on exercises and lecture materials of which every piece is a response to certain opportunities and limitations. What kind of budget are they working with? What kind of material resources (e.g., labs) are available? How much time is there to impart crucial information? Who are their students, and how many are there? Based on an awareness of the environment and their audience, skilled supervisors and professors assemble the pedagogical tools that will do the most good for the greatest number of learners.

Online educational activities have been among those tools for decades now, so in one sense, they're nothing new. But the advent of highly sophisticated interactive learning objects marks a qualitative break with the online educational activities of the past. Today's ILOs are more than just complex delivery vehicles for didactic information; they are, rather, highly versatile and accessible arenas that, if designed well, can impart the same things to learners as lab- or field work. In effect, ILOs are capable of containing all or nearly all elements of a supervisor or professor's pedagogical *bricolage*.

We used the phrase "designed well," which suggests a lot but explains little, because by now our readers are doubtless aware that a well-

137

designed ILO is one that embeds an instructor-expert's *tacit* knowledge in its very mechanics. Learners coming away from a well-designed ILO will (perhaps without even realizing it) be in possession of not only a set of data, but also a web of associations and habits that correspond to the associations and habits of a professional with extensive real-world experience. Therefore, the value of sophisticated, well-designed ILOs as pedagogical tools cannot be overestimated.

It requires no special inspiration or prescience to see that well-designed ILOs will come to be a cornerstone of education in both the corporate and academic worlds; if you're in the field, you know that it's already happening. The less-obvious but altogether critical observation is that the ascendant complexity and sophistication of ILOs requires a shift in the process by which we create them. Instructional designers, software developers, program managers, project managers, graphic artists, instructor-experts, and the variety of other contributors to ILO initiatives must adopt both the spirit and strategies of *micro-collaboration*. It is only through micro-collaboration that any ILO will be able to achieve its full potential as a powerful and highly accessible teaching tool. That's why the five factors laid out in this book are so important: they are what make it possible for us to transform emerging technology into platforms for reaching real people who can make a difference in the real world.

Which is to say that in the end, the five factors are all about the learner. Just as every ILO should be.

References

Ackerman, M., V. Pipek, and V. Wulf. 2003. *Sharing expertise: Beyond knowledge management.* Cambridge, MA: MIT Press.

Aldrich, C. 2011. Designing sims the Clark Aldrich way. Manuscript in progress; quoted with permission.

Allen, Michael A. 2003. *Michael Allen's guide to eLearning.* Hoboken, NJ: John Wiley.

Argyris, C. 1991. Teaching smart people how to learn. *Harvard Business Review* (May/June): 99–109.

Bacharach, S. 2006. *Keep them on your side: Leading and managing for momentum.* Avon, MA: Platinum Press.

Beck, K., M. Beedle, A. van Bennekum, A. Cockburn, W. Cunningham, M. Fowler, J. Grenning, et al. Manifesto for Agile software development. agilemanifesto.org (accessed 23 April 2011).

Berge, Z. 1995. Facilitating computer conferencing: Recommendations from the field. *Educational Technology* 35: 22–30.

Bolman, L.G. and T.E. Deal. 2008. Reframing organizations: Artistry, choice, and leadership. San Francisco, CA: Jossey-Bass.

Botturi, L. 2006. E2ML: A visual language for the design of instruction. *Educational Technology Research and Design* 54(3): 265-293.

Chacon-Moscoso, S., M.T. Anguera-Argilaga, J. Antonio, P. Gil, and F.P. Holgado-Tello. 2002. A mutual catalytic role of formative evaluation: the interdependent roles of evaluators and local programme practitioners. *Evaluation* 8(4): 413-432. http://evi.sagepub.com/content/8/4/413.abstract

Collins, A. and R. Halverson. 2009. *Rethinking education in the age of technology: The digital revolution and schooling in America.* New York: Teachers College.

Duning, B., M. Van Kekerix, and L. Zaborowski. 1993. *Reaching learners through telecommunications.* San Francisco, CA: Jossey Bass.

Egenfeldt-Nielsen, S. 2006. Overview of research on the educational use of video games. *Digital Kompetanse* 1(3): 184-213.

Fargnoli, M., E. Rovida, and R. Troisi. 2006. *The Morphological Matrix: Tool for the development of innovative design solutions.* ICAD. Http://www.axiomaticdesign.com/technology/icad/icad2006/icad2006_21.pdf

Fitzpatrick, J., J. Sanders, B. Worthen. 2003. *Program evaluation: Alternative approaches and practical guidelines.* Allyn & Bacon.

Flagg, B.N. 1990. *Formative evaluation for educational technologies*. Hillsdale, NJ: Erlbaum.

Gee, J. P. 2003. *What video games have to teach us about learning and literacy*. New York, NY: Palgrave Macmillan.

Halverson, R. 2004. Accessing, documenting, and communicating practical wisdom: The phronesis of school leadership practice. *American Journal of Education*, 11(1).

Hokanson, B. 2007. *The handbook of visual languages for instructional design: Theories and practices*. Hershey: IGI-Global.

Inglis, A. 2003. Facilitating team-based course designing with conceptual mapping. *Distance Education* 24(2): 247-263.

Knox, A. B. 2002. *Evaluation for continuing education: A comprehensive guide to success*. San Francisco: Jossey-Bass.

Kuniavsky, M. 2003. *Observing the user experience: A practitioner's guide to user research*. San Francisco, CA: Morgan Kaufmann.

Merriam, S. and R. Caffarella. 1999. *Learning in adulthood: A comprehensive guide* (2nd ed.). San Francisco, CA: Jossey-Bass.

Nerur, S., and V. Balijepally. 2007. Theoretical reflections on Agile development methodologies. *Communications of the ACM* 50(3): 79-83.

Pfotenhauer, J., D. Gagnon, M. Litzkow, and C. Blakesley. 2009. *Designing and using an on-line game to teach engineering*. Paper presented at 39th ASEE/IEEE Frontiers in Education Conference, October 2009. San Antonio, TX.

Salo, O., K. Kolehmainen, P. Kyllonen, J. Lothman, S. Salmijarvi, and P. Abrahamsson. 2004. Self-adaptability of Agile software processes: A case study on post-iteration workshops. *Lecture Notes in Computer Science* 3092: 184-193. Retrieved from Springer Link database.

Schank, R. C. 1990. *Tell me a story: A new look at real and artificial memory*. New York, NY: Charles Scribner.

Squire, K. 2005. Game-based learning: An XLearn perspective paper. Masie Center eLearning Consortium.

Squire, K. 2003. Design principles of next generation digital gaming for education. *Educational Technology* (September/October).

Talby, D., O. Hazzan, Y. Dubinsky, and A. Keren. 2006. *Reflections on reflection in Agile software development*. Paper presented at Agile Conference (April).

Tessmer, M. 2002. *Planning and conducting formative evaluations*. London, England: Kogan Page.

University of Wisconsin-Madison. (2011a) Engage: Transforming teaching and learning through technology. http://engage.wisc.edu/index.html.

University of Wisconsin-Madison. (2011b). Simulations and Games, evaluations. http://engage.doit.wisc.edu/sims_games/evaluation/index.html (accessed 23 April 2011).

University of Wisconsin-Madison. (2011c). Meeting notes, Cool-It. https://wiki.doit.wisc.edu/confluence/display/coolit/Meeting+Notes (accessed 23 April 2011).

Index

D

Davis, Sarah, 134-136

Deal, Terrence E. (*see also* Boman, Lee G.), 19, 24

organizational dynamics theory, 24-25, 125

deliverable, 67

design blueprint, 85, 99

Dietz, Amy, 43, 44, 67

didactic overload, 91

didactic pedagogy, 16, 32, 40, 55-56, online learning, 91-93

dialectic pedagogy. *See* interactive pedagogy.

documentation, 71-72, 83-86, 98-102

DoIt Wiki, 80, 97

double-loop learning, 76

E

educational outcomes. *See* learning outcomes.

Edwards, Kathleen M., 64-66

egalitarian team atmosphere (*see also* flattening power relationships), 73, 91

Engage Program, 21, 32, 61
CSB, 103-107
Cool-It, 32, 33, 43
formal evaluation, 114, 116
iterative devolvement, 77

exemplars, 95, 104

explicit knowledge, 17-18, 91
definition, 17-18

F

Five Factors of Micro-Collaboration. *See* Aleckson's Five Factors.

flattening power relationships, 19
autocratic instructor-expert, 50, 53-54
communication, 88, 91
dismissive instructor-expert, 50, 53
IDD team strategies, 50, 51-58, 64-65
In Practice, 64-66
instructor expert strategies, 58-59, 64-66

manager strategies, 60-62
momentum, 127-128

formal reflection, 76, 130

formative evaluation, 20, 109-117
Agile development, 74, 75-77
benefits, 111-112
Cool-It, 37, 114
definition, 109
Engage program, 114, 116
formalizing, 112-114, 130
In Practice, 118-121
momentum, 130, 131-132

formative evaluation, formal, 112-114
In Practice, 118-121

formative evaluation, informal, 112-113
problems with, 116

G

Gaines, Meg, 134-136

Gagnon, Dave, 33, 59-60, 67, 79, 95-98, 114-115
as project manager, 79-81

game-design theory, 27

game-based learning, 39-41

H

Howles, Lee, 51, 77-79, *78*, 103-107

HRER (Human Resources and Employment Relations) 43, 44, 45

Hughes, Brad, 103-017

I

IDD (instruction design and development)
experts, 14, 16
professional devolvement, 51-53

IDD team
responsibilities, 44, 51-52, 91
relationship with instructor-expert, 49-51, 53-54

ILO (interactive learning objects)
assessment, 36, 45-47
definition, 14, 15-16
graph of complexity, 16, *17*, 31
pedagogical tool, 36-37